1996

HEDDA GABLER

Gender, Role, and World

Twayne's Masterwork Studies
Robert Lecker, General Editor

HEDDA GABLER

Gender, Role, and World

Charles R. Lyons

Twayne Publishers • *Boston*
A Division of G. K. Hall & Co.

Twayne's Masterwork Studies No. 62

Copyright 1991 by G. K. Hall & Co.
All rights reserved.
Published by Twayne Publishers
A division of G. K. Hall & Co.
70 Lincoln Street
Boston, Massachusetts, 02111

First published 1990.
10 9 8 7 6 5 4 3 2 1 (hc)
10 9 8 7 6 5 4 3 2 1 (pb)

Library of Congress Cataloging-in-Publication Data

Lyons, Charles R.
    Hedda Gabler : gender, role, and world / Charles R. Lyons.
        p.   cm. — (Twayne's masterwork studies ; no. 62)
    Includes bibliographical references and index.
    ISBN 0-8057-9417-4 (alk. paper). — ISBN 0-8057-8141-2 (pbk. :
alk. paper)
        1. Ibsen, Henrik, 1828–1906. Hedda Gabler.   I. Title.
II. Series.
PT8868.L96 1990
839.8′226—dc20   90-43607
                                                                            CIP

For Leila, once again

Contents

Note on the References

Quotations from *Hedda Gabler* are from *The Oxford Ibsen*, vol. 7, edited by James Walter McFarlane (London: Oxford University Press, 1966). This version was translated by Jens Arup. Page numbers follow the citation. In some instances, I note how I would translate differently. For my own working translation of the original text, I have used *Ibsens Samlede Verker*, vol. 3 (Oslo: Gyldendal Norsk Forlag, 1962). I have used the original spelling of the characters' names throughout. I identify the unmarried Julle Tesman and Diana as Frøken Tesman and Frøken Diana.

Henrik Ibsen.
Engraving by Bork, ca. 1890

Chronology:
Henrik Ibsen's Life and Works

1807   Hegel publishes *Phenomenology of Mind.*

1828   Henrik born to Knud and Marichen Ibsen of Skien, Norway.

1835   Knud Ibsen, who runs a general store and importing business, suffers financial losses; with their four children the Ibsens move to their country home in nearby Venstøp.

1843   Søren Kierkegaard publishes *Either—Or.*

1844   Becomes an apothocary's apprentice in Grimstad, a small, isolated town of fewer than one thousand inhabitants.

1846   Fathers an illegitimate son, Hans Jacob Henriksen, with Else Jensdatter, a servant in the apothocary's household ten years his senior.

1850   His first play, *Catiline,* based on Roman history, is published just before he leaves Grimstad to move to Christiania (Oslo) to begin university studies. His second play, *The Warrior's Barrow,* a romantic nationalistic drama, is produced at the Christiania Theater in late September and repeated twice in the autumn.

1851   Takes a position as playwright-in-residence at Norwegian Theater, Bergen.

1852   Writes *St. John's Night,* which was produced in Bergen the next year. Later he would forbid publication of the play, which combines prose and verse, during his lifetime. He assumes new duties as director in Bergen.

1855   Publishes *Lady Inger of Ostraat,* his first play entirely in prose. With *St. John's Night* and *The Warrior's Barrow* it fails in production at the theater in Bergen. Ibsen directs a Norwegian adaptation of Shakespeare's *As You Like It* in September, and in November lectures on Shakespeare and his influence on Scandinavian literature.

1856   Produces *The Feast at Solhaug* under his own direction at the Bergen theater as part of a program of reviving interest in Norwegian folk literature.

1857   In January the theater at Bergen produces *Olaf Liljekrans*, which anticipates *Peer Gynt* in verse style and some content, in an unsuccessful production. Ibsen becomes artistic director of the Norwegian Theater in Christiania in September.

1858   Publishes *The Vikings at Helgeland* in which he attempts to imitate the style of the sagas and produce a drama that celebrates Norwegian nationalism. Marries Suzannah Thoresen, an attractive twenty-one-year-old with an interest in drama whose father is the Dean of Bergen.

1859   Son Sigurd is born.

1862   Publishes in December *Love's Comedy* set in contemporary Norway but written in rhymed verse.

1863   Publishes in October *The Pretenders* (with the erroneous publication date of 1864), a historical drama set in Norway in the thirteenth century. This play anticipates the epic scale and complexity of the next stage of his work. Applies for an annual national pension as a poet, but the Storthing (the Norwegian Parliament) denies his request.

1864   Encountering serious aesthetic, bureaucratic, and financial problems in his work as a stage director and playwright, grows disenchanted with the theater. Decries the restricted scenic facilities of the nineteenth-century theater. His lack of success as a playwright intensifies his growing alienation from the practical processes of stage production. Manages to accrue sufficient funds to remove himself from Norway and travels to Italy (via Copenhagen, Berlin, and Vienna).

1864–1867   In the first years of his chosen exile ignores the restrictions of theatrical performance and writes the first two of his three large-scale dramas for an audience of readers rather than spectators: *Brand* (1866) exercises the kind of radical revision of traditional Christian ideology that Kierkegaard voices, and *Peer Gynt* (1867) provides a kind of picaresque alternative. With *Emperor and Galilean* in 1873, these widely disparate texts constitute extended, philosophically oriented works that complement and contrast with each other in an intricate interrelationship. Both *Brand* and *Peer Gynt* have become major works in the modern repertory.

1865   John Wilkes Booth assassinates Abraham Lincoln 14 April at Ford's Theater in Washington, D.C., an event that provokes

Ibsen to write a poem condemning the hypocrisy of the wide-spread grief that followed this event.

1867   Karl Marx publishes *Capital*.

1868   The Ibsens leave Italy for Dresden.

1869   John Stuart Mill publishes *The Subjection of Women*. Ibsen returns to the project of writing for the theater with *The League of Youth*, a political satire in colloquial language that, during Ibsen's lifetime, would remain popular in Norway.

1872   Nietzsche publishes *The Birth of Tragedy*.

1873   With *Emperor and Galilean* Ibsen abandons writing poetic drama. This massive text dramatizes the conflict between Christianity and paganism that divides the consciousness of the historical figure of Julian, using an idea of history as dialectic that reflects Hegel's ideology. Despite the implicit irony that underlies the three large-scale epic dramas and often questions their heroes' motives, the fact that their protagonists strive to achieve a Faustian comprehension of reality relates the plays to the romantic dramas of Goethe as well.

1875   The Ibsens move to Munich. Ibsen travels to Berlin to see the famous company of Duke Georg II of Saxe-Meiningen perform in a limited production of *The Pretenders*. Here Ibsen encounters the most extraordinary theater of the time, one that influenced the development of realism with its innovative integration of mise-en-scène and text. Publishes *Pillars of the Community*. With this play he begins to deal seriously with contemporary subjects, writing a work that functions as an experimental prototype of the kind of dramatic realism that the next sequence of work would refine progressively.

1879   Publishes *A Doll's House* in early December, which proves very successful in print and premieres in Copenhagen on the 21st. The character of Nora, who leaves husband and children to find her own life, is based on the real Laura Kieler. The play is produced successfully in Stockholm, Christiania (Oslo), and Bergen early the next year.

1880   The Ibsens return to Italy.

1881   Publishes *Ghosts*, in which Fru Alving leaves her husband, returns to him at the urging of the man she loves, Pastor Manders, and later bears a son who inherits his father's syphilis. Because of the content of this work, Ibsen becomes the object of extreme controversy and vitriolic attack as an immoralist.

1882   Nietzsche publishes *The Gay Science*. *Ghosts* has its American premiere in Chicago in June. Publishes *An Enemy of the People* in November, a play that focuses on Dr. Stockman, who refuses to compromise when he discovers the baths, which are the chief economic resource of his town, are polluted and dangerous.

1884   Publishes *The Wild Duck*, which he views as a departure from his previous work, an ensemble play that balances the comic and the tragic in examining the strategies in which its characters create fictions about themselves to deal with painful experience.

1885   The Ibsens move to Munich.

1886   Publishes *Rosmersholm*, an intense, sharply focused drama that represents a pair of repressed lovers and addresses free-thinking, incest, and apostasy. This is the play that Sigmund Freud would address analytically in 1914. To Ibsen's disappointment, the play receives a hostile response. In December Duke Georg II of Saxe-Meiningen successfully produces *Ghosts* with Ibsen present, but the censors forbid its public performance in Berlin.

1887   Antoine founds Théâtre Libre in Paris, a small experimental theater devoted to the new realism.

1888   Publishes *The Lady from the Sea*, which displays its heroine, Ellida Wangel, emotionally tied to the sea and the memory of her youthful brief relationship with a young American. The man returns and she must choose between her husband and this mysterious lover. The play baffles and confuses critics and readers. Swedish playwright August Strindberg publishes *Miss Julie*, reinforcing the growing strength of the new realism.

1889   Otto Brahm opens the Freie Bühne in Berlin with *Ghosts*, founding a theater devoted to a program similar to the Théâtre Libre.

1890   In July George Bernard Shaw presents a lecture on Ibsen to the Fabian Society that is to become the basis of *The Quintessence of Ibsenism*. Ibsen publishes *Hedda Gabler* in December to the worst press reception he has ever received.

1891   In January *Hedda Gabler* premieres at the Residenztheater in Munich. In February Eleanora Duse plays Nora in *A Doll's House* in Milan. In March J. T. Grein opens the Independent Theatre Society in London with *Ghosts* in an attempt to bring the avant-garde spirit of the Théâtre Libre and the Freie Bühne to London. In July the Ibsens return to live permanently in Christiania (Oslo).

1892   According to an unconfirmed report Ibsen meets his illegitimate son for the first and last time when the man petitions him for money. Publishes *The Master Builder* in December, which many consider his finest play. This text explores the psyche of a middle-age builder who confronts the erotic presence of a strange young woman who comes to claim a promise she says he made to her ten years earlier.

1894   In April Aurélien Lugné-Poe produces *The Master Builder* at Théâtre de l'Oeuvre, the Parisian theater that vied with Théâtre de Libre as the principal seat of the avant-garde in Paris. Later in the month the famous actress Réjane plays Nora at the Théâtre Vaudeville in Paris. In December Ibsen publishes *Little Eyolf*, in which he continues his exploration of responsibility, sexuality, and guilt in a play that achieves commercial success in its early sales.

1896   Publishes *John Gabriel Borkman*, which, using older characters and his retrospective technique, details the relationship of a failed capitalist to the two women, twin sisters, who mark the choices he makes in life.

1898   The Moscow Art Theater produces Anton Chekhov's *The Sea Gull*, which first played in St. Petersburg in 1896, under the successful direction of Konstantin Stanislavski.

1899   Publishes his final play, *When We Dead Awaken*, which explores the reunion of an aging sculptor with the model whom he renounced years earlier. Gives the play the subtitle "A Dramatic Epilogue," which refers not to the idea that this will be his final play but, rather, suggests that he intends to move even further from the qualified realism of this play into newer forms of drama. Freud publishes *The Interpretation of Dreams*, with erroneous date of 1900.

1900   In January *When We Dead Awaken* has its first performance in Stuttgart, Germany, followed almost immediately by performances in Copenhagen, Helsinki, Christiania (Oslo), Stockholm, and Berlin.

1901   Suffers a stroke.

1902   The first Nobel Prize for Literature is awarded to the French poet Sully-Prudhomme, ignoring Ibsen, Tolstoy, Chekhov, and Hardy.

1906   Dies 23 May. The Norwegian government gives him a state funeral 1 June.

1907   Norway is the first European sovereign state to establish universal female suffrage.

1914   Suzannah Thoreson Ibsen dies 3 April.

Literary and Historical Context

Michael Gross and Kate Mulgrew in the Mark Taper Forum production of *Hedda Gabler*, in a new version by Christopher Hampton, at the James A. Doolittle Theater in Hollywood, 1986. *Photograph by Jay Thompson*

1

The Historical Moment

With the publication of *A Doll's House* in 1879, Henrik Ibsen began to attract an international audience, and his plays were appropriated by avant-garde theaters in France, Germany, and Great Britain. The series of plays from *A Doll's House* through *When We Dead Awaken*, which was published in 1899, belongs as much to the aesthetic and social histories of the Continent, England, and America as they do to Scandinavia. With these plays as hallmarks of both the new realism and the new symbolism, the theatrical avant-garde became an international movement that drew key theatrical figures into a network and marked the boundaries between the conventional, established theater and the self-consciously experimental performances of the art theater.

Ibsen's dramatic texts in the 1880s and 1890s assume the ethical program of repositioning the criteria of moral decisions from the residual doctrines of orthodox theology and traditional morality to the kind of material utilitarianism that John Stuart Mill advocates. For example, the hypocrisy in which males invoke Judeo-Christian morality to confine women and sustain their own freedom and authority circumscribes the experience of Nora Helmer in *A Doll's House*, Fru Alving in *Ghosts*, Rebekka West in *Rosmersholm*, and Hedda in

Hedda Gabler. Torvald's self-justification, the egocentric rationalization of Pastor Manders, the variation of this self-serving orthodoxy in the speeches of Kroll, Johannes Rosmer's brother-in-law, provide intensified images of bourgeois self-explanation that would edge on the satiric if they did not define the destructively narrow morality that social norms exert upon Ibsen's more idealistic protagonists. Judge Brack's clear articulation of the difference between what conventional people say and what they do informs a culturally self-defining matrix against which Hedda's suicidal gesture defines itself as both an extraordinary act and a social transgression.

Erich Auerbach, the author of the influential *Mimesis,* argued that Ibsen's realistic drama is inextricably grounded in the social dynamics of his moment and, as well, that this involvement in significant issues contributed, in some degree, to "the complete transformation of the social status of the *bourgeoisie.*"[1] *A Doll's House, Ghosts,* and *Hedda Gabler* provided resonant theatrical images that participated in the cultural redefinition of women's place in European society. These plays offered their ideology in immediately accessible theatrical images that posed the possibility that people in the audience could also participate in societal change.

Actors identified with the social program of Ibsen's drama and became part of the liberal community's demand for change. In an article dealing with the kind of critical intelligence Ibsen demanded of his early actors, Gail Gibson Cima writes, "The Ibsen actors needed an open-minded attitude toward their characters' morals. Any actress, for example, unable to perceive a justification for Nora leaving Torvald, or for Hedda's suicide, would be unable to play either character."[2] Cima's quotation of the following passage from an appendix to *The Quintessence of Ibsenism* points out Shaw's identification of the difference between the actresses who originated Ibsen's major female roles in England and their counterparts in the more commercial, orthodox theater:

All four [Janet Achurch, Florence Farr, Marion Lea, and Elizabeth Robins] were products of the modern movement for the higher education of women, literate, in touch with advanced thought, and coming by natural predilection on the stage from outside the theatrical class, in contradistinction to the senior generation of inveterately sentimental actresses, schooled in the old fashion if at all, born into their profession, quite out of the political and social movement around them—in short, intellectually naive to the last degree.[3]

The American Elizabeth Robins, who produced and acted in a series of Ibsen performances in London, must have perceived a symbiotic relationship between the politics of her career and dramas that seemed keyed to the same issues that directed her professional work as an actress and producer. Ibsen's texts exercise the intellectual strategies through which this moment defined itself as significantly transitional, and it is appropriate that Ibsen, a Norwegian, became the signal playwright of the age. Norway self-consciously addressed the position of women and was the first European sovereign nation to establish female suffrage in 1907. In 1882 women were admitted to the University at Christiania (Oslo); and in 1884, a petition, signed by Ibsen, was presented to the Storthing to give married women a right to property and earnings.

While Auerbach credited Ibsen for "giving a style to the serious bourgeois drama," he devalued the lasting status of these plays because he believed that the social changes they demand had been accomplished by 1914. Auerbach's judgment belongs to the period immediately after World War II and, therefore, does not respond to the recognition in the past twenty years of the distance the women's movement has yet to travel. While we can value his description of the dialectic between text and social transition in Ibsen's work, we can see that the plays sustain both an ideological and aesthetic immediacy that negates his assumption that history has accomplished the principal reforms the playwright sought. More accurately, perhaps, the dynamics of change itself, as a phenomenon of Ibsen's moment and our own, attracts our attention to these texts.

Hedda Gabler first appeared in 1890, relatively late in the sequence of Ibsen's realistic plays. The earlier plays in this series formulated the structural conventions of the new dramatic realism.[4] This innovative style attempted to build a fresh relationship between performance and audience by establishing a precise alignment between the socioeconomic detail of the plays and the spectators' own experience, by using dialogue to present a frank examination of social issues from a liberal bias and by displaying pyschological motivation indirectly through behavior. This style eliminates extended passages of self-revelation and direct address to the audience, and limits the representation to dialogue that accompanies or embodies uninterpreted behavior. These texts attempt to present an image of objectivity; and yet they also involve the subjectivity of the spectator in the unspoken, subtly suggested inner life of its characters. Dramatic realism displays the fascination of the late nineteenth century with cause in the exploration of the dynamics of the interaction of determining past and troubled present. The biological principles of heredity, the tenets of psychology, the cultural matrices of conventional morality, and the laws of economics combine in Ibsen's plays to form patterns of fate and nemesis that assume the functions filled by the supernatural in classical tragedy. Consequently, the structures of determinism in the plays are conventional but the dynamics work themselves out in mundane situations with which the audience could identify directly. In other words, the illusion of realism in Ibsen's plays derives from a carefully arranged series of references, linguistic and visual, that relate the action to those categorical systems by which its spectators interpreted actual experience. Members of the original audience were able to locate the scene—almost invariably a bourgeois domestic interior—within their direct knowledge of similar environments; relate the behavior of the characters to contemporary theories of psychology and biology; and identify the motives, status, and experience of the characters as consistent with their own economic position and the principles that they assumed governed modern western European societies. In other words, those texts we identify as realistic appear as vulnerable to explanation according to those systems of determinism as comparable data from actual experience do.

Ibsen's realistic texts translate the minutia of scenic description and the ostensibly objective examination of human behavior that characterize the novels of Flaubert and Stendahl into the briefer, less expansive, and more tightly organized limits of dramatic texts and performance. With a surface clarity equal to the novels, these dramas display the implicit restrictions of a culture that counters their heroes' dreams and aspirations and implicates them in a capitalistic economy in which they function either as exploiter or exploited. Ibsen's realism places characters in recognizable financial crises with material specificity. In *A Doll's House*, Nora forges a check in order to gain the money needed to restore her husband's health, and her final action, her departure from her husband's home, places her in economic jeopardy because she has no means to support herself. In *The Wild Duck*, Ibsen contrasts the affluence of the bourgeois Grösserer Werle with the poverty of the family of his former partner, Old Ekdal. The Ekdals, surreptitiously supported by Werle, have been disenfranchised, economically and socially by a crime that Ekdal shares with Werle. In *The Master Builder*, the protagonist has moved from the artisan class to the haute bourgeoisie, both by his skill and the resources, in real property, that he attains by marriage into a wealthy family. In *John Gabriel Borkman*, the text shapes its protagonist's romantically demonic vision in the historically accurate language in which nineteenth-century capitalism idealized and justified the exploitation of natural resources. These dramas work out their complications through the commonplace fiscal instruments of mortgages, loans, wages, commissions, annuities, and inheritances. The significance of financial risk in *Hedda Gabler*, as a condition of life, informs my discussion of the dynamics of economic exchange. While Ibsen's plays represent extraordinary events in the psychic history of his characters, they locate these occurrences within common social and domestic transactions that seem on the surface to be metonymic of a repetitive sequence of ordinary moments that precede the dramatized action.

Part of the power of Ibsen's drama derives from the phenomenon of suppressing the emotionality of extreme psychic crises to fit within the acceptable limits of middle-class public behavior. Today, of course, that restraint marks the difference between the sensibility of Ibsen's moment and our own and reads, to us, as typical either of the artificiality of late-nineteenth-century dramatic language or the behavior it attempted to represent. We need to recognize, however, that, within Ibsen's time, his discussions of incest, venereal disease, sexual exploitation, and illegitimacy—even within those circumlocutions we find strained—shocked his audiences and made him an infamous international celebrity. Ibsen's fame, and notoriety, were the consequence of both a radical aesthetic and an equally radical ideology.

While Ibsen's plays represent the political and ethical schism between the authority of traditional institutional structures and the cultural revolution that was reorganizing European society, he firmly denied any formal affiliation with socialism. He declared that in his representation of human character he had reached the same conclusions that the moral philosophers associated with the Social Democrat party had gained through their research.[5] While Ibsen wished to be seen as a force within the social changes taking place, he did not want to be perceived as the agent of any political or social organization or to be intellectually dependent upon the ideas of others. Ibsen's letters and public statements voice the kind of fierce determination to identify the self as both unique and extraordinary that marks the language of the characters in his plays. Consequently, whereas Ibsen's dramas voice the liberalism of his age as statements of clear assertion as well as irony, the playwright himself frames those ideas as the expression of his own subjective vision.

The absence of divine intervention in the human experience represented has become a commonplace in discussions of modern drama. Discussions of what makes modern drama "modern" often cite Nietzsche's proclamation of "the death of God" in *Die fröliche Wissenschaft* (*The Gay Science*) in 1882 as the ideological signal point that marks the difference between pre-modern and modern tragedy. The arbitrariness of periodization, of course, has become a factor in recent criticism; we now find it difficult to identify an assumed belief in the Judeo-Christian God in *King Lear* and equally difficult to avoid recognizing a "modern" theological skepticism in Euripides. Using the emergence of world economic systems as a basis for modernism, we have come to think of Renaissance drama as "early modern." The absence of divine intervention in theatrical texts and the emphasis upon natural rather than supernatural determinism precedes the drama of the nineteenth century, and it isn't primarily the absence of God in Ibsen's plays that motivates their innovation. We recognize now, of course, the basic artifice of the conventions in which Ibsen organized his representation of social, psychological, and economic processes, and we understand that realism itself constitutes various schemes of representation, not the actual verity of the behavior and scenes presented on the stage. In other words, these texts situate their characters in communities, social classes, rooms, or topographical sites that the spectator would identify in relationship to the scenes of his or her own experience; and these dramatic figures articulate their desires and fears—which, from a distance, do not differ in kind from those of an Oedipus, Hamlet, or Phèdre—in language that uses the values of their nineteenth-century world. We can, however, mark the radical materialism of Ibsen's realistic drama as the basis of their innovation. Whereas Ibsen's plays enact the conventional situations of serious drama—the clash of generations, the competition between ideology and pleasure, the conflict between individuality and community—the action works itself out through the materially represented social, political, economic, moral theories in which late-nineteenth-century European society examined itself.

The specificity of scene and its cultural immediacy set the new realism apart and stimulated audiences to see these plays as "new." George Bernard Shaw attempted to make Ibsen into the radical social reformer that the British critic, novelist, and playwright believed himself to be, and Shaw's enthusiastic endorsement of Ibsen's sociopolitical program caused critical perception of the Norwegian to be biased for decades. However, we should not disallow Shaw's claim that audiences saw themselves in Ibsen's plays.[6] The illusory replication of contemporary society and place—their concrete specificity—must have provided a major source of interest, intrigue, and aesthetic pleasure for the original audiences of Ibsen's plays. That topical interest, of course, determined the plays' immediate appeal and yet, in some sense, masked the equally seductive power of their language. That same topical materialism distances present audiences from the social situation of their action; and, as we scan these texts to identify their current appeal and seek new modes of performance, we read through the specific social circumstance to some ideological or psychological action that, while it may use the language of the late nineteenth century, is not exclusively confined by it. As we work with an Ibsen text now, either in analytic study or production, one of our tasks is to identify the play's historical contingency in relation to its mode of enactment. Ibsen's realistic works are aesthetically dependent upon their representative mode: the belief that the objective world can be approximated on the stage of a theater and in the behavior of actors. At the same time, the plays contend with the idea that a focused vision of reality can be contained within the psychological, temporal, and spatial limits of theatrical performance. That very contention, which displays an aesthetic in crisis, ties the plays to their moment and also makes them relevant to us as we continue to struggle with the idea of representation, immediacy, and the relationship of performance to cultural moment.

2

The Importance of the Work

Hedda Gabler has been consistently one of Ibsen's most popular plays in performance. Strong, intelligent, and articulate actresses have claimed the title role throughout its history: Elizabeth Robins, Nazimova, Eva La Gallienne, Maggie Smith, Ingrid Bergman, Janet Suzman, Glenda Jackson, and Kate Mulgrew. Because it addresses questions of male and female sexuality, language, and gender, as well as society's determination of both sexual role and personal identity, *Hedda Gabler* has become as significant a play for the close of the twentieth century as it was for the end of the nineteenth. Our increasing understanding of these issues as cultural phenomena that impact our experience as well as inform the literature of the past gives special value to a text that has both intrigued and confounded spectators and critics since its first performances. The character of Hedda Gabler puzzles spectators because this character is enigmatic in ways different from the more accessible figures of Halvard Solness and Johannes Rosmer. The play intrigues us more because of its atypicality than its similarity to Ibsen's other popular realistic plays. The text is intricately implicated in Ibsen's highly unified body of work and, simultaneously, stands apart from those other dramas.

The theatrical shock of Hedda's suicide provides one of those theatrical transgressions that never fails to surprise us, even if we are familiar with the text. Robert Egan's 1986 production at The Mark Taper Forum removed the back wall of the inner room and displayed the dead Hedda against the white wall of the garden, blood splayed across its surface. While this visual strategy broke through Ibsen's careful stage directions, it reified that initial shock and reestablished the suicide as a violent and transgressive act. Hedda's suicide provides one of the reasons the play intrigues us, both in the theater and in criticism. Here, in this specific action, Ibsen uses the material he works and reworks through his playwriting and yet, in this text, that familiar event, through reconfiguration and reemphasis, became surprising, innovative, and original.

Hedda's suicide does, of course, repeat a recurrent phenomenon in Ibsen's writing, the sacrificed female. Consider these examples: the death of Agnes in *Brand;* the desertion of Solvig in *Peer Gynt;* the suicide of Hedvig in *The Wild Duck;* the suicide of Beate in *Rosmersholm;* Borkman's renunciation of Gunhild in *John Gabriel Borkman;* Allmer's renunciation of Asta in *Little Eyolf;* and Rubek's renunciation of Irene in *When We Dead Awaken* and her perception of herself as "dead." In many instances, the text aligns the renunciation of the female with the death of a child: Alf in *Brand*, the metaphoric child of Eilert's manuscript in *Hedda;* the child Eyolf in *Little Eyolf;* the metaphoric child of the statue, Resurrection, in *When We Dead Awaken.* However, the plays that hold these examples focus on a male protagonist as their central figure. The loss of the female and the death of the child is something that happens to the heroes; and these male protagonists use these events to conceptualize their experience and define their identity. Hedda's self-sacrifice, however, is demanded by Eilert's failure to commit an aesthetic suicide only indirectly, and this act is not subject to the extended presentation of the male it affects. Instead, the play closes quickly on the event, without even the brief discussion that resolves *The Wild Duck,* where Relling predicts that Hedvig's suicide will become transformed in the empathic story that Hjalmar will tell. Hedda's death does not become an event to be narrated by its hero; on the contrary, Hedda's act—as *spectacle*—focuses our attention on its immediacy, its nature as a self-sufficient and complete performance, its function as an assertion of Hedda's vision of herself—not in language—but in a deed that others will see as a vivid physical image. Despite some analogies with other Ibsen plays, the ending of *Hedda* exercises a different dramaturgy, one that remains atypical of the playwright's practice.

Hedda Gabler continues to attract readers and spectators for another reason as well. The play combines the representation of a strikingly compelling central figure with the presentation of an intricately complicit social group. That is, the play reveals a group of figures engaged in individual projects of self-definition that involve the others in destructive cross-purposes. Tesman and Eilert direct themselves in searches for an identity through vocation, in behavior that echoes the action of earlier and later male protagonists in the canon. The play focuses upon Hedda, however, as she implicates the others in her scheme to build or to sustain her identity; and, as a female, this protagonist does not have the instrument of a vocation to use in forming her image of the self. Ibsen's male protagonists use the professional project—religion, architecture, art, philosophy, and the writing of history—to formulate a comprehensive vision of reality. In *Hedda Gabler,* the play concentrates upon a protagonist who does not have this resource, who cannot project an image of the self as the author of a history or the creator of some aesthetic artifact.

The male heroes of Ibsen's plays are identified by the text they write or the works they produce; and, as well, they fight against the strictures of those narratives or artifacts that freeze their identity as the manifestations of their egos. The processes in which Ibsen shows his female hero forging an identity in different ways deserve close attention. The failure of Ibsen's heroes to resolve the conflict between the desire to hold the world in a static vision and the impulse to surrender to sensual and sensuous experience frames the hero's quest in an ironic skepticism. In *Henrik Ibsen: The Divided Consciousness,* I discussed that conflict as a tension between the protagonist's personal vision of reality, which I identified as *myth* and the material realism of concrete phenomena, the flux of life. Here, I saw the hero's vocational project as the manifestation of the desire for form and the attraction toward sexuality as a representation of the competing impulse to realize the self in sensation. Ibsen's texts do not vacillate between materialism and idealism but, rather, focus upon the tension between conceptual and physical strategies of defining the self:

> In Ibsen, reality is incomprehensible, and the attempt to compre-
> hend it is an attempt to enclose and contain that which cannot be
> held in any structure. The myth of comprehension is an illusion of
> being able to contain in space what cannot be restricted within
> spatial organization—the temporal processes of phenomenal experi-
> ence. However, to abandon this myth is to abandon the concept of
> the self, the notion of continuity, and even the concept of structure
> itself. To experience phenomena without a mythological formal con-
> cept is to give up the idea of the self and lose that identification in a
> sensual flux.[1]

Hedda Gabler exercises the typical Ibsenian plot only if we place Eilert as the male figure of the triad completed by Hedda and Thea. As the argument of this book demonstrates, the shift in focus caused by rotating that triad to emphasize one of the females is not merely another way of telling the same story. Rather, the rotation transforms the narrative and discloses the pain of a different experience. However, despite the playwright's insight, the figure of Hedda Gabler remains prominently displayed in the space but often the activity of her mind remains outside of our focus. While Hedda is acutely self-conscious and sustains a performance of the persona she wishes perceived, the text does not reveal the character in extensive private moments of self-analysis. The text and its performance build an image of a clever, manipulative figure who attempts to exploit skillfully the identity the males project upon her and, at moments, to reject the restraints of that imposed value. That is, she functions as a screen on which the men who surround her attempt to write their versions both of her and of themselves. Ibsen's male heroes have the language to write their own narratives, projecting antithetical identities on the pair of women who define their potentiality and reveal their guilt, even if they must eventually confront the speculative, hypothetical, and ultimately illusory nature of their professional missions. Ibsen prohibits Hedda from making that kind of effort and practicing that kind of self-analysis, delusive or not. In *Hedda Gabler,* Ibsen does not withhold the possibility for a satisfying life from his female protagonist because she is a female. His plays hold no promise for sustained satisfaction and creativity for women *or* men. In this play, however, he withholds the primarily material to search for personal identity from this dynamic woman— even if her search, like those of the male protagonists, would remain futile and, ultimately, self-destructive.

The figure of Hedda Gabler Tesman attracts and repels. That combination of identification and estrangement contributes to the lasting fascination of this work. The text and its performance voice the need to change the position of women in the social world it projects and, simultaneously, subvert that project in two significant ways: first, in depicting its central figure as a woman who destroys herself and her unborn child to sustain her sense of identity; and second, by denying sustained creativity to any figure in that world. *Hedda Gabler*'s representation of its female protagonist shares in the late-nineteenth-century project of redefining the role of women in society and, simultaneously, restricts that redefinition within an ideology that sustained a patriarchal program. The complexities of its representation of gender and social structure provoke us to reassess this text—and its continued appeal—with the greater understanding of the representation of gender our moment commands. Similarly, the different modes of dramatic representation that have developed since the original performance of this play—the combination of referential detail and significant lacunae that we find in Beckett, Pinter, and Shepard—allow us to address the ellipses and occlusions in *Hedda Gabler* with a fresh perspective. *Hedda Gabler,* therefore, functions in this moment as a key text in our project of understanding the transition between the realist and anti-realist theater, the representation of gender at the end of the nineteenth century, and the correlation between that moment's articulation of sexuality and our own.

3

Critical Reception

A work such as *Hedda Gabler,* which has received the status of a modern classic, sustains two interrelated but independent lives: as a script for theatrical production, adapted to the performance conventions of the moment; and as a text to be read, analyzed, and integrated into the current project of literary or aesthetic theory. The reception of the play, therefore, depends upon the strategies of aesthetic perception implemented at a particular moment and the shifting emphases that are brought to the foreground as both the conventions of the theater and literary analysis change. Dramatic criticism has subjected the text of *Hedda Gabler* to a variety of different readings in the past century. As I claim in my introduction to *Critical Essays on Henrik Ibsen,* the work of any major writer functions as a screen on which the dynamics of evolving aesthetic theories display themselves.[1]

Ibsen published *Hedda Gabler* at the beginning of the 1890s, the very moment at which his reputation as a realist was solidifying. At this point in his career, Ibsen's fame, ironically, derived from the response to works he wrote several years earlier, texts subtly different from his writing in this play. In the late 1880s and early 1890s, Ibsen's rapidly growing international audience thought of him principally as the radical author of *A Doll's House,* which celebrated a young woman's exit from husband, home, and children, and *Ghosts,* which focused on inherited syphilis as physical evidence of the implicit corruption of bourgeois morality. While his writing was moving away from the more overtly social realism of *A Doll's House* and *Ghosts,* Ibsen's public persona remained caught in his image as a radical writer who had brought a new authenticity of character and social environment to the stage in order to clarify significant social issues from a progressive point of view. Ibsen was the first playwright who was adopted by an international avant-garde that advocated a progressive aesthetic and political program. *Ghosts* opened Otto Brahm's Freie Bühne in 1889 and also provided the premiere production for J. T. Grein's Independent Theatre Society in 1891. Both the Freie Bühne and Grein's London theater patterned themselves self-consciously on Antoine's Théâtre Libre. This influential organization itself performed the Parisian première of *Ghosts* in late May 1890 in the tiny Théâtre de Menus Plaisirs with Antoine himself as Oswald.

While *Hedda Gabler* clearly relates to the realistic texts that precede it, the work refuses to yield the biographical detail that informs the spectator's image of the protagonist in the earlier plays from *Ghosts* onward. Because the public view of both Ibsenian drama and Ibsenism remained tied to the style and content of these plays, Ibsen's experimentation in *Hedda Gabler* puzzled its initial audiences and readers. The play disturbed these spectators who found its female protagonist to be eccentric, abnormal, and disturbingly disconnected from any counterpart in reality. As biographer and translator Michael Meyer translates the review by Georg Göthe in *Nordsik Tidskrift,* "The whole characterization of the play is obscure. . . . [The characters] are alive, but only to a degree; deep inside them there is something abstract, cold, dead."[2] In a review of a performance of Hedda by Elizabeth Robins, Henry James revealed his discomfort with his inability to fix the playwright's characters within a conventional series of "types." "Sometimes [Ibsen] . . . loses sight too much of the type-quality and gives his spectators *free play* to say that even caught in the fact his individuals are mad. We are not at all sure, for instance, of the type-quality in Hedda."[3] While *Hedda Gabler* seemed, on the surface, to be stylistically consistent with the realistic drama of the plays that precede it, its specific violations of that form shocked and discomfited its early audiences.

From our perspective late in the twentieth century, Ibsen's canon displays a Janus-like position in dramatic history. The early plays look backward toward both Shakespearean historical drama and its romantic nineteenth-century variants. The early and middle realistic plays appropriate several of the structural conventions of the Scribean well-made play and transform this popular structure into the highly specific representation of event and scene that constitutes the dramatic style we identify as realism.[4] This period in Ibsen's work held sway over the avant-garde briefly, and then serious experimental theater diffused the empirical project of realism early in the twentieth century in the experiments of expressionism, symbolism, and surrealism. While we see the difference in Ibsen's later plays as an extension and transformation of the principles of realism and identify their participation in the development of antirealistic drama, some of Ibsen's early critics saw the style of the later sequence from *Hedda Gabler* to *When We Dead Awaken* not as formally different but, rather, as flawed examples of the kind of writing he had produced earlier. Using the earlier plays as criteria, many, including William Archer, Ibsen's English translator, did not understand the ways in which the later plays move away from the strictures of realism.

The discrepancy between the public notion of Ibsenism in the early 1890s and the style of the playwright's writing at that moment demonstrates the potential any innovative text holds to puzzle its original audiences. Understandably, the public evaluates the new work within the terms of their previous experience of dramatic works in general and the works of the individual playwright in particular. George Bernard Shaw, of course, contributed a great deal to shaping the reception of Ibsen in the English-speaking world. In July 1890 he delivered the famous lecture on Ibsen to the Fabian Society that was to become the basis for *The Quintessence of Ibsenism*.[5] His misapprehension of Ibsen's playwriting has become a commonplace in the later

Ibsen criticism that celebrates its dramatic language. However, we need to recognize that Shaw's image of Ibsen as a realist who used dramatic dialogue as an instrument to examine critical social problems does correspond to the literal style of the plays of the 1880s and the very ideas that made them seem both daring and innovative in the 1890s. Shaw did not metamorphose an apolitical poet into a socialist as later criticism suggests. The plays do, indeed, detail the kind of liberal thinking Shaw identifies and celebrates; however, Shaw's enthusiasm for his own perception of this ideology blinded him to the subtlety, equivocation, and irony of the language of Ibsen's drama. Shaw's vision of Ibsen is not wrongheaded but, rather, partial. The Englishman's emphasis on Ibsen as polemicist ignored both Ibsen the poet and Ibsen the ironist, who undercut his liberalism with a skepticism toward any human assertion.

Theater practitioners, of course, recognized Ibsen as a poet earlier than critics did. When Aurélien Lugné-Poe broke away from Antoine's Théâtre Libre to form the symbolist program of the Théâtre de l'Oeuvre, Ibsen became as much a vehicle of his agenda as he had been for Antoine's celebration of realism.[6] Despite Lugné-Poe's incorporation of Ibsen into the symbolist movement, early critical commentary on Ibsen followed Shaw's direction and discussed the plays as social documents and exemplifications of the theater's new ability to replicate the world of social reality. At first, of course, Ibsen's plays were discussed in newspapers and journals, as the events of the day. Later, in the period between the world wars, Ibsen became a subject for more academic study. When serious criticism addressed *Hedda Gabler,* most commentary treated the play as a dramatized tract on the plight of women, emphasizing the frustrated intelligence and creativity of its heroine. Combined with the response to *A Doll's House,* the reception of this play firmly identified Henrik Ibsen as a playwright whose significance derived from his ability to represent social issues within the new mode of theatrical realism.

The idea that Hedda's brilliance is circumscribed and repressed by a society in which all authority is held by men dominates commentary on the play. George Bernard Shaw wrote to Elizabeth Robins after seeing her performance of the character: "You were sympathetically unsympathetic, which was the exact solution of the central difficulty of playing Hedda."[7] Shaw's comment capsulates the conventional perception of this character: the intelligent, energetic, potentially creative woman whose limited opportunity for self-development and self-expression directs her into exploitative and destructive action.

One difficulty with this conventional view of the character of Hedda Gabler is the fact that this figure's isolation—her inability or unwillingness to access the world of ideas—contrasts problematically with Ibsen's representation of other dynamic women. For example, Mrs. Alving, trapped within the morals of a restrictive society, liberates herself intellectually as she reads and studies the works of those free-thinkers whose ideas influence Ibsen. Rebekka West, confined by class and society to work within domestic tasks, incorporates Dr. West's progressive ideology and conceptualizes her work with Rosmer as part of an educational movement to free the populace from bourgeois morality. Hedda, on the other hand, identifies herself through the restrictions she confronts and limits herself to the role of General Gabler's daughter. While she envies Løvborg's rebellious behavior, she sustains no interest in the intellectually radical content of his writing. She is complicit in her entrapment.

Ibsen himself was uncomfortable with feminism's appropriation of his playwriting, but we need to temper his attempt to distance himself from this political program with our awareness of his unwillingness to identify himself with any external agent or influence. Ibsen rejected being publicly identified with any political movement or ideological source. While both the issues and developing methodologies of feminist criticism may help us to deal with Ibsen's play, one other principal fact argues against seeing the text as a feminist tract: the play presents a complexly interconnected group of female and male characters caught in economic and social jeopardy, figures whose aspirations are thwarted by the strictures of their society, the dynamics of their own psyches, and the destructive impulses of others. While the play brings the figure of its protagonist to the foreground, Ibsen's text presents this woman locked in dynamic interaction with the members of a clearly defined social group, each of whom is victimized by a culture whose economy determines their function and value.

Clearly, the figure of Hedda Gabler Tesman, suggested by the language of the text and sometimes embodied in the skilled performance of an actress, displays an energy that fascinates readers and spectators; and yet, more than in any other Ibsen text besides *The Wild Duck, Hedda Gabler* is the drama of an intricately involved group whose experience constitutes "a perverse dance."

Despite the fact that *Hedda Gabler* isolates its characters and displays them only in the confines of the public area of the Falk Villa, the rigid social codes and economic laws of the European world at the close of the nineteenth century determine the coordinates in which Ibsen contrives the action of his drama, the behavior of his characters, and the language they employ. When Inge-Stina Ewbank discusses the language of Ibsen's women in a persuasively argued essay, she reaches the conclusion that Ibsen's language, spoken by both males and females, is a language of the oppressed. Professor Ewbank uses the strategies of sociolinguistics to reveal the ways in which Ibsen's spare dialogue represents the operation of societal restraints upon his dramatic characters. Interestingly, when the important early commentator Edmund Gosse criticized the lack of clarity in *Hedda Gabler,* he marked the mimetic value of the play's terse speech. Ironically, Gosse's negative assessment of this dialogue, which marks the *realism* of the language, identifies an aspect of the text that we now perceive as positive. Gosse asserts: "In the whole of the new play there is not one speech which would require thirty seconds for its enunciation. . . . It would add, I cannot but think, to the lucidity of the play if some one character were permitted occasionally to express himself at moderate length, as Nora does in *A Doll's House,* and as Mrs. Alving in *Ghosts.* . . . On the stage, no doubt, this rigid broken utterance will give an extraordinary sense of reality."[8] Gosse senses the difference between the amount of expository detail in Ibsen's earlier realistic plays and the absence of extended retrospection in this text. The negative comments of early critics, such as Gosse and Göthe, actually isolate aspects of the play that depart from the conventions of realism more clearly than those who appropriated Ibsen into the ranks of polemists. However, scholarship tied Ibsen to realism despite the fact that the theater had already responded to the antirealistic aspects of his later drama.

Even though Ibsen's texts were vulnerable to the kind of symbolist production Lugné-Poe created and Gordon Craig envisioned in his designs of *Rosmersholm* for Eleanora Duse, dramatic criticism itself did not have a methodology to deal with the implicit poetry of Ibsen's dramatic language until after the New Critical revolution in Shakespeare studies gave value to the interconnections of imagery that provide a different notion of dramatic structure than the organization of character and action. Muriel C. Bradbrook, a specialist in English Renaissance drama, led the reappraisal of Ibsen's dramatic language, using analytic techniques developed in Shakespearean criticism.[9] John Northam's brilliant explication of *Hedda Gabler* in *Ibsen's Dramatic Method* relates the text to the visual details of scene. This essay demonstrates the increased sensitivity to language and performance and considers performance as a complicated and yet significant movement through a series of interrelated images.[10]

When the emphasis in Ibsen criticism shifted from the sociopolitical focus defined by Shaw to the analysis of language prompted by the development of the New Criticism, interpretations based upon the connection between the text and its historical moment seemed both reductive and old-fashioned. As well, the sociopolitical readings seemed to respond naively to the realistic mode, assuming, as they appear to, that the objective of the texts is the manifestation or expression rather than the interpretation of a segment of the European ideology. Even as sophisticated an intellectual history as Brian Downs's *Ibsen: The Intellectual Background* tends to assume that Ibsen's texts reflect various ideological positions rather than participate in either the formulation or critique of the ideas they confront.

Reviewing the more formalistic interpretations of Ibsen that range from Muriel Bradbrook's application of the principles of the New Criticism to my own phenomenologically oriented study, I would point out that these discussions of the plays do not take their mode of representation into sufficient consideration. While both Inge-Stina Ewbank and I analyze the processes in which the demands of making the metaphoric structure of the language plausible within the terms of realism invests the individual image with intensified and amplified significance, neither of us takes into sufficient account the aesthetic experience in which the spectator perceives the physical and social scene as an aesthetic substitute for the world of his or her own experience. That is, while the more formal interpretations of Ibsen's plays have isolated the conventions of realism as *conventions,* as artificial and contrived as the conventions of expressionism or symbolism, formal studies have not focused enough on what I would now identify as the *aesthetic game* of realism.

Whereas we would like to think of the history of commentary on a major work as a reflection of a growing understanding of the text, we need to confront the validity of Edward Said's assertion that "criticism, not less than any other text, is the present in the course of its articulation."[11] That is, the critical interpretation voices its moment in history rather than reembodying the voice of the text as the past. In the present moment, we value especially two phenomena in the dramatic text: We confirm the power of its intricate and keenly self-referential language to build an image of a specific and unique world in performance and, we recognize the ways in which that language and the world it images is itself the product of a specific cultural moment. We need to confront self-consciously the fact that we see both the dramatic text of *Hedda Gabler* and the cultural past in which it originated with the biases and concerns of this moment. We need to look at this play not merely as an artifact in our study of dramatic history but rather as an aesthetic phenomenon that lives in the theater and in our private imagination in the present. We need to exercise our awareness of the problematics of defining role by gender and identify the ways in which sexual differentiation directs the text of this play. We need to place the text in two temporal moments, identifying the ways in which its language of word and gesture both refracts and judges its own cultural moment and allows us to perceive both this past and our present.

As an area of specialization in dramatic literature, which itself is a subject within the larger field of literary studies, there is often a delay between the articulation of innovative critical theories and their application to individual playwrights such as Ibsen. Ibsen studies, for example, did not incorporate the methodologies of the Shakespearean New Criticism developed in the 1930s until after World War II. It will probably take a few years before Ibsen's realistic plays receive the kind of commentary that the New Historicism began to mark out for Shakespeare in the 1980s. In the immediate future, Ibsen criticism will need to address the development of dramatic realism as a project in which certain aspects of the dominant ideology are confirmed and other aspects subverted. We need to understand more fully the appropriation of Ibsen's texts by the avant-garde in France, Germany, Great Britain, and the United States as a particular cultural exchange in which the new dramatic form of realism, the liberal politics of the plays, and the aesthetic and ideological projects of these small companies combined to mark out the territory of a new kind of theatrical enterprise: an ideologically committed art theater. We shall need to think more carefully about the ways in which Ibsen's texts moved from these experimental theaters—which have become historically significant but which, in their moment, operated on the periphery of the commercial theater—to their place in the standard repertory of major theaters.

The relationship of the text of *Hedda Gabler* to the project of feminism one-hundred years ago and the feminist critique at the end of the twentieth century reveals the difference between the two historical moments. Ibsen's plays share in the examination of the limitations imposed upon women at the end of the nineteenth century; and yet Ibsen's own view of women was itself circumscribed within his celebration of their primary role as the nurturing mothers whose mission is to educate the young. When Ibsen addressed the Women's Rights League, he distanced himself from their program and, as well, limited his celebration of women to their role in the nurturing and discipline of children. Ibsen's view of women expressed in this statement undercuts the assertion of Hedda's suicide. As critic Errol Durbach writes in his discussion of the playwright's ironic representation of romanticism:

Hedda in finally asserting her self also sunders that self in a grotesquely literal manner, from history in its most organic, most palpable form. Her unborn child dies with her—the living counterpart of the symbolic "child" which she burns in a fit of jealousy and triumph at the end of Act III. The future history of civilisation perishes twice in Ibsen's play. And in this act of perverse negation, Hedda's Romantic selfhood stands condemned in its barrenness.[12]

For the 1990s, we need to address Ibsen's representation of women and the social world not only in terms of his historically determined ideological program but also as a text that allows us to think about the issues of gender as they articulate themselves today.

A Reading

George Deloy and Kate Mulgrew in the Mark Taper Forum production. *Photograph by Jay Thompson*

4

The Problem of Interpretation

At this moment in the history of literary theory, the commentator faces a series of difficult choices in writing an essay that puts forward the "reading" of a text by a prominent author. Structuralism, poststructuralism, and particularly the predications of Michel Foucault have put into question the idea of the text as the manifestation of the unique subjectivity of an author, and any attempt to deal with writing in terms of human agency seems to implement a fallacy of intentionality. Criticism has became sensitive once again to the relationship between texts and historically determined ideologies. But, compared to the earlier, more positivist historicism, the recent orientation in literary studies sees the text engaged in history in a greater reciprocity—not expressing a zeitgeist but involved in the production and reproduction of specific components of ideology.[1] East German scholar Robert Weimann provides a model for that kind of cultural exchange in *Shakespeare and the Popular Tradition in the Theater:* "The sensibilities and receptivity of the [Elizabethan] audience and consciousness and artistry of the drama were so mutually influential that a new historical synthesis seems conceivable only through an increased awareness of the dialectics of this interdependence."[2] While Weimann speaks specifically about seventeenth-century British theater, his description of the dialectical relationship between stage and society in the formation and transmission of ideology provides a useful model for the equally transitional moment of the late nineteenth century, when the avant-garde theater articulated many of the critical issues involved in the liberal reformation of European culture. The new orientation in historical criticism, with its feminist component, alerts us to the value of seeing texts both as the reinforcement of the values of the dominant patriarchal culture and as subversive social instruments, embodying more unorthodox voices, in a progressive critique of that culture.

Ibsen's realistic plays, as I have noted earlier, locate their action within ordinary daily transactions of European bourgeois life. These texts and their performance present themselves in specific, tangibly perceptible physical and social phenomena. In that sense, they reinforce aesthetically scientific and philosophic attempts to relate to the world through the processing of empirical evidence. Ibsen's "realism" does not actually reproduce the objective world of the late nineteenth century, but these texts define themselves according to certain conceptual processes in which a particular liberal, progressive imagination at the end of the nineteenth century would organize a vision of the world. Much of the criticism that identifies Ibsen as "the father of dramatic realism" puts forward the naive notion that the theater did, indeed, approximate the real world in an increasingly authentic ability to match the world of the spectator's experience. In *Criticism and Ideology*, Terry Eagleton makes an arresting corrective point in his discussion of Dickens. He claims that a work such as *Bleak House* does not represent "Victorian England," but rather "certain of Victorian England's ways of signifying itself."[3] Ibsen's realistic texts do not signify through an increased empirical authenticity, but they articulate specific assumptions with which the liberal community at that moment predicated the world.

One of the problems of looking at Ibsen's realistic plays as a screen upon which key issues within a cultural revolution display themselves is that this methodology encourages us to consider these texts as if they were authored anonymously, as if they were the products of history writing itself. As we confront the sequence of Ibsen's realistic dramas, we need to address both their assimilation of an ideology of social change and the ways in which they organize themselves through an idiosyncratic and relentlessly constant fascination with a paradigmatic sexual triad: a male who defines himself, in part, by his relationship to two women, an aggressively erotic female and a submissive, erotically neutralized female. Ibsen's movement into the realistic mode marks a clear relationship between his writing and certain key aspects of the ideology that was reshaping modern Europe. And yet, the development of the material specificity in which these texts operate does not radically transform what we could call the psychosexual paradigm with which he structured the relationship of his principal characters. The fact that Ibsen's plays from *Catiline* in 1849 to *When We Dead Awaken* in 1899 tend to exercise a particular sexual dynamic, despite the diversity in their mode of representation, complicates our perception of the relationship between a play such as *Hedda Gabler* and the liberal critique it appears to voice. Throughout fifty years of writing, Ibsen's imagination held on to a particular sexual triad that catches the past and present of the male hero in a pattern of eroticism and renunciation. In his earliest extant text, *Catiline,* written when he was twenty-one, Furia, the vestal virgin who tempts the hero, reembodies the presence of her sister, Thalia, an innocent young woman who killed herself years earlier after being raped by Catiline. Here, in a prototype of the process of substitution that repeats throughout the plays, Furia's reenactment of the virginal but erotic appeal of her sister proves disastrous to the hero. Furia presents an image that is antithetical to Aurelia, the patient wife who encourages Catiline to withdraw from his confrontation with Cicero. The text ignores, to a large degree, the historic confrontation between Catiline and Cicero that provides its ostensible subject, and focuses upon the political drama as the consequence of the hero's movement between two females: the dutiful and submissive wife and the aggressive young woman who comes to Rome to enact revenge for her sister's death. Catiline's action responds less to his political objective than to the erotic presence of this dynamic woman. The pattern of sexual renunciation, sacrifice, and substitution in this play repeats itself throughout the canon. The consistency of this psychosexual paradigm, which seems to direct the formal structure of Ibsen's dramas, argues against approaching the plays exclusively as discrete, individualized interactions with the evolving social dynamics of the second half of the nineteenth century.

Whereas there are compelling reasons to perceive *Hedda Gabler* as the articulation of the sensitivity of Christiania's (Oslo's) attention to the status of women and the difficulties of forging social change, the clear relationship between this play and Ibsen's *The Vikings at Helgeland*, written over thirty years earlier, complicates any attempt to isolate the immediate historical circumstance as an originating impulse. The playwright declared that he wrote *Vikings* under the influence of Petersen's translations of Icelandic Sagas. Here he juxtaposes two pairs of men and women that clearly function as prototypes of the two principal couples in *Hedda Gabler*. The structure of the plot and its characters implement the same sexual dynamics as the later play despite the fact that the playwright self-consciously positions the figures of the earlier play in an epic scene and inextricably ties the later four figures to their late-nineteenth-century bourgeois environment and the audience's awareness of the position of women as a significant social issue.

The Vikings at Helgeland contributes to the nationalistic movement that attempted to define Norway both as a discrete political entity and as a culture independent of Denmark and Sweden. Petersen's Icelandic family sagas and M. B. Landstad's publication of Norwegian folk ballads gave Ibsen both an idea of content and images of style for *The Feast at Solhaug* and *The Vikings at Helgeland*. Ibsen forged a mode of representation for *The Vikings* that attempted the opposite of his later realism.[4] He sought a dramatic form that would function as a contemporary equivalent to the scale, objectivity, and detachment of the formalized epic. And this project—like the later realism—he perceived as related to a sociopolitical dynamic: the reinforcement of Norway's perception of itself as an independent political and cultural presence in Scandinavia. Both this impulse toward a nationalistic drama and the later attempt to unite content and form in a vitalized realism demanded innovative dramas that were, formally, slightly beyond the immediate experience or competence of his audience. In both *The Vikings* and *Hedda Gabler,* however, Ibsen conflated his attempts to configure a new dramatic style with an obsessive reworking of his essential drama. As we address the ideology of *Hedda Gabler* and the nationalistic program of *The Vikings,* we need to recognize that Ibsen used the ideas of society in each play to represent the familiar sexual drama that almost each Ibsen text enacts.

The Vikings at Helgeland opposes the strongly willed, forceful Hjørdis with her foster sister, the sensitive, passive Dagny; and this play contrasts the heroic, virile warrior Sigurd with his foster brother Gunnar, who is more compassionate and less egocentric. In the narrated past of the play, Hjørdis, already an epic-size heroine, is guarded by an enormous white bear. To win her, a man must kill this animal. Sigurd is attracted to her, but he withdraws in favor of Gunnar, who loves Hjørdis. Gunnar, afraid of battling with the bear, convinces his foster brother to kill the animal. He does and makes love to the awestruck Hjørdis. She leaves with Gunnar, thinking that he is the man who has conquered her. Sigurd marries the mild Dagny. Years later, when Sigurd provokes a quarrel between the foster brothers, the angered Dagny reveals to Hjørdis that her marriage has been based upon a lie, that it was Sigurd who conquered the bear. Hjørdis and Sigurd reveal their love for each other. Hjørdis attempts to persuade Sigurd to kill Gunnar, but he convinces his foster brother to fight in single combat. Sigurd realizes that if he kills Gunnar, Hjørdis will be required, by ancient law, to kill him. Hjørdis believes that she and Sigurd can be united only in death and wounds Sigurd fatally. Before he dies, Sigurd destroys her belief that they will be joined in death by confessing that he has become a Christian. In despair, Hjørdis kills herself by casting herself over a cliff into the sea.

The Vikings at Helgeland dramatizes the convoluted relationship of two couples in which the vital, extraordinary man and woman marry the less vital partner. Hjørdis, the brilliant female, appropriates the male strength of an epic hero in a destructive course that rechannels the energy of her love for Sigurd. Hjørdis's powerful will, restrained by Ibsen's representation of those epic values that make her secondary to her husband, works itself out in destructive, exploitative, manipulative acts; and, when she is unable to structure the death of the man she loves according to her own vision, she kills herself. Hjørdis, in that sense, is as confined by these *archaic* values as Hedda is by the restraints of late-nineteenth-century middle class society. Of course, we could easily argue that Ibsen's transcription of epic values is, itself, produced by the same culture that underlies the society he represents as the social scene of *Hedda Gabler*. In any case, when Ibsen published the second edition of *The Vikings at Helgeland* in 1883, he admitted that he was drawn to this particular saga because of its dynamic contrast between two women.[5] However, when Ibsen self-consciously attempted to explore and to display the social dynamics of the contemporary Scandinavian bourgeoisie, his dramatic figures operate within the same parameters of restraint and freedom that function in his equally self-conscious representations of archaic history. Even more significantly, these figures from the nineteenth-century bourgeoisie fulfill the same behavioral paradigms as do their epic prototypes.

The basic dynamics of relationship and the behavior of the dramatic figures in *Hedda Gabler* do not derive from the material specificity, the realist mode, in which Ibsen presents these figures. The play's consistent use of the basic sexual paradigm clarifies that the topical grounding in contemporary detail constitutes the mode or medium of its representation. The materially rendered scene—the precisely positioned human community of *Hedda Gabler*—is not the object of imitation, but, rather, an aesthetic instrument by which the complexly shifting configuration of its dramatic figures is given theatrical presence and immediate accessibility. The dramatic character, Hedda, is not determined merely by the social restrictions imposed upon the female at the end of the nineteenth century as that world is represented by the social dynamics of the play; the character is also configured by the social dynamics of Ibsen's basic sexual paradigm, a sexual paradigm that voices the male-dominated sexual ideology of Ibsen's moment in history mediated through the idiosyncrasies of his own psyche.

The course of Ibsen's playwriting is a history of productive assimilation. That is, his writing appropriates both formal structures and details of content and absorbs them into the basic sexual paradigm. The imaginative power of that essential triad dominates the process of assimilation; and the complexity and detail of the adapted material enrich and strengthen the paradigm. Michael Meyer documents the playwright's use of personal knowledge and experience in both the pathos of Laura Kieler's relationship to the text of *A Doll's House* and the ambiguity of Emilie Bardach's relationship to the figure of Hilde Wangel in *The Master Builder.* What should be of interest here is not the biographic source of the details of character and plot in these cases but, rather, the processes in which specific details become contextualized within the basic paradigm. The medium of the realistic mode, the materiality of representation, constitutes the most significant assimilation of material into the fundamental structure of the sexual triad.

Ibsen's realist texts (and performances of them) demand that we perceive them from two principal perspectives simultaneously. First of all, they challenge us to respond to them as mimetic, as detailed, objective examinations of human behavior that proceed from the empirical strategies of their own moment. They ask us to process the data that the text and its performance provide us in order to build our own images of their plausibility and reliability. Simultaneously, however, the texts demand that we attend to them as aesthetic constructs, intricately sequenced experiences in time. These structures embody interconnections that transcend plausibility, presenting relational patterns that are, in this sense, irrelevant to the mimetic project, and put forward a sense of the work as a highly organized aesthetic object in itself.

The specific terms that Michael Fried develops in his study of the paintings of Thomas Eakins in *Realism, Writing, Disfiguration* allow us to differentiate between our acquiescence to the rules of Ibsen's mimetic referentiality and our recognition of the text as the product of an aesthetic organizational scheme. In using the artifact of a painting, Fried offers an analysis that has some analogy to the realistic spatial scene of an Ibsen text in performance. Fried distinguishes between two forms of perception that Eakins's painting stimulates. He identifies the perceiver's awareness of the aesthetic organization of the painting as pictorial perception and the antithetical perception of the realism of the painting as graphic or "the participatory mode of perception."[6] To borrow these terms, I would assert that Ibsen's realistic plays in general and *Hedda Gabler* in particular demand a response that incorporates both a submission to their graphic or representational function and a recognition of their intricately contrived schematization of that material. The more formal studies of Ibsen attend well to the pictorial aspects of the texts but tend to ignore our response to the graphic quality of the dramas. As well, the studies of Ibsen, like Shaw's commentary, that address principally the graphic or representational suppress our recognition of their pictorial nature, the aesthetic processes that mark the texts as created structures.

Ibsen's realistic dramas attempt to provide graphic representations or theatrical substitutes for highly individualized images of typical, upper-middle-class Norwegian domestic sites by using highly referential architectural detail, furniture, and decorative objects. The original audience would have read the totality as a specific environment that is keyed to the protagonist and is, at the same time, both the consequence of his or her economic status and the indication of that position. In part, Ibsen's texts represent his character's relationship to a normative scale of values through the dramatization of the character's conscious and unconscious relationship to this scene. For example, Hedda's deprecating perception of the Falk Villa and its furnishings and her uncontrollable sense of alienation from its atmosphere provide a significant and signifying dynamic as we witness her mediated perception of the fictional place embodied by the theatrical scene.[7]

Beginning with *Pillars of the Community* and moving through *John Gabriel Borkman,* Ibsen used the increasingly facile scenographic resources of the theater and the potential for referentiality in dramatic language to posit an aesthetic image that appeared to correspond to the world of the spectator's experience. That is, the physical spaces the fictional figures inhabit, the clothes they wear, the objects they use and refer to, the language they speak, the socioeconomic relationships they are subject to, their familial and sexual relationships, the emotional and intellectual strategies they use in conceptualizing their experience—each of these facets of representation displays itself in relationship to the intended spectator's sense of the normative. That is, each of these signifying units presents itself in relationship to the received scale of values that underlay the systems of architecture, decoration, fashion, social behavior, and language with which the spectator would have perceived his or her own experience of the objective and social world. Each reference to the empirical categories of interpretation that the spectator would recognize, and the accumulated patterns of reference, would work to build aesthetic images of figure and ground that the spectator would extrapolate and build into an image of character and society related to his or her own experience. In a sense, the realistic character—or the graphic representation of character—functions as an objective image to the degree that the dramatic figure can be placed on an implied grid within the coordinates of socioeconomic, geographic, psychological, and biological markings. In that sense, the chart of an individual character produces a sense both of his or her typicality and uniqueness.

Individual spectators recognize that the image on the stage is false in the sense that it is an artifice established for the performance; but, because it sets itself up as a distilled or intensified substitute for the kind of figure they would encounter outside of the theater, they perceive and judge it, at least in part, with the same conceptual or evaluative strategies they would employ outside of the theater. The playwright of the realistic text, therefore, relies both upon the spectator's conscious and unconscious use of codes of categorization, including the assumptions about psychology made by the audience in its perception of the dramatic figure.

Because the playwright builds an image of character and place that the spectators should recognize as a unique, highly particularized image that corresponds to the objective world of their own experience, the conventions of realism demand that the moment represented in the realistic play be roughly, at least, coextensive with the moment of performance. The playwright assumes and exploits two hypothetical worlds: the created fiction or illusion and the spectator's perceived reality. While the writer may extend or refine the spectator's perception of objective reality, he works within the general scientific, historical, psychological, and sociological beliefs of the moment. The hypothetical construction that the spectator perceives as *reality* is, of course, a transitive hypothesis subject to the sequence of discoveries, corrections, and remappings of the world that mark our understanding of the physical and social sciences.

The realistic play, as realism, therefore, "holds in perfection but a little moment" and quickly outdates itself as realism, because the phenomenon of coincidence between the hypothetical world of the fiction and the hypothetical world of the spectator's perception of reality is finite. An audience, one generation removed from the moment of the play, may view its fictional world as the reproduction of a *former* moment, perceiving the characters of that removed time as distanced participants in a self-contained epoch that the study of history has processed as isolated and distanced from the present. The assumptions of a present historiography will filter their perception of the dramatic characters as characters. That is, the spectators who view these figures will judge them as constrained by the coordinates of the previous moment in history and, also, will judge the assumptions on which the playwright created them as a function of the historical moment. In other words, the spectator's recognition that the idea of *character* in the play is itself historically determined will distance the dramatic figure and bring its nature as an artificial construct to the foreground. For realism to function as realism—and not historical drama—the arena in which the action plays itself out must use, at least approximately, the hypothetical coordinates in which the spectators perceive their world. If individual spectators perceive too great a discrepancy between the fictional scene and the hypothetical reality they formulate as the world of their own experience, they will identify the relationship between theatrical scene and the world as one constituted by metaphor or analogy. In that sense, the significance of the represented scene derives from the meaning invested in that discrepancy or difference. Within those terms, I would agree with Auerbach that Ibsen's plays no longer maintain their energy as realistic confrontations with social issues because they no longer align directly with the immediate ideas that structure the spectator's social concerns. And, certain specific elements of the text, which contain outdated assumptions about empirical detail, point out the discrepancy between what is *real* to the 1880s and what is *real* at the close of this century. For example, in *Ghosts,* Ibsen translates the orthodox notion of the visitation upon sons of the "sins of the father" into the modern phenomenon of physiological inheritance, Oswald's infection by his father's syphilis. We now recognize that this phenomenon is biologically impossible, that the only way that Oswald could have become infected with his father's disease would have been for the father to have infected his wife, who would have transmitted the disease to Oswald at his birth. Consequently, in this text, the image of inherited disease no longer functions as a pseudoaccurate empirical datum but must be attended to as a metaphor of the corruption of the father that manifests itself upon the body of the son despite the young man's sexual innocence.

For today's audiences, Ibsen's realistic plays function as historical dramas because of the impossibility of matching the fictional world they inhabit with the hypothetical reality their audiences perceive as their own experience of the objective world. However, our evaluation and analysis of these texts can speculate about the coincidence between Ibsen's dramatic scenes and their own moment in history. At some level of conscious playwriting, Ibsen used the theater's potential for establishing an aesthetic equivalent to the specific material presence of the objective world. In that sense, the image of the world of the play, as a fictional reality established in performance, continues to function as a kind of self-reflexive substitute for the world of the spectator's experience to the degree to which that past world may be reinhabited imaginatively. The nonmimetic criticism of the past generation tends to ignore that aspect of Ibsen's writing. That is, as it focuses on the individual object or paradigm, the analysis does not deal with the dominant stylistic convention of realism itself. In dealing with latent content, this kind of critical discourse ignores the accumulation of detail, the processes in which that detail builds specific networks of referentiality, and sees instead the detail as part of a metaphoric system rather than a system of categorization that the spectator uses as he would in analyzing the objective world outside of the theater. In other terms, the conventions of realism in the sequence of plays from *Pillars of the Community* to *The Master Builder* present a scene that identifies itself as a substitute, a theatrical equivalent to an actual place, that appears to be unmediated, unprocessed by aesthetic criteria. The scene, the physical space, and the behavior of the figures who appear within it—all appear uninterpreted. However, the pictorial function of our response recognizes that the objective world of these texts is, indeed, a highly mediated construct.

The subjective aspect of that mediation argues against seeing these texts as autonomously as the strategies of poststructural analysis would prefer. To extrapolate from Anthony Gidden's critique of post-structuralism, the human agency of Ibsen's idiosyncrasy constitutes too great a presence as we work with these plays. While Giddens acknowledges the contribution that structuralism and poststructural-ism have made to "our understanding of cultural production," he offers the following critique as he describes the emphasis upon reading in the decentering strategies of recent theory:

> Writing is sometimes portrayed as though texts wrote themselves; the relegation of the author to the role of a shadowy adjunct to writing is manifestly unsatisfactory. We might accept the signifi-cance of the theme of decentring of the subject, and therefore the need to construct what an "author" is. But we shall have no proper grasp of the process of writing unless we manage to recombine satisfactorily the elements that have been decentred. Structuralism and post-structuralism have in my view been unable to generate satisfactory accounts of human agency, . . .; and this weakness reap-pears in the shape of the tendency to equate the production of texts with their inner "productivity."[8]

In this study of *Hedda Gabler* I attempt to deal with both the graphic and the pictorial functions of the text and, in that joint objective, to attend to the play as a document in cultural production as well as a production of a human agent, as a variation of Ibsen's powerful and idiosyncratic representation of the sexual paradigm that dominates his writing.

While the specific editorial charge of this book is to produce a "reading" of Ibsen's *Hedda Gabler,* the sequence of chapters that follow do not attempt to persuade readers to accept a single, highly unified, wholly cohesive statement of the meaning of the text. In the following chapters I attempt to examine in some detail the processes in which Ibsen's provocative text organizes itself to produce a series of interlocking theatrical images. My objective has been to reveal the internal logic of the play as it uses the techniques and conceptual paradigms of its moment to build a theatrical event. When I use a grammatical construction such as "the text organizes itself," I am not trying to use such predication to avoid the currently unpopular assignment of intention to the writer. I am also not trying to remove "human agency" from the project of writing *Hedda Gabler.* Various and complex determinants operate within Ibsen texts: the ideological paradigms he inherits, those he self-consciously develops, those to which he is subject un-self-consciously. One of the paradigmatic structures to which Ibsen is clearly subject is the sexual triad of a man and two women, a structure of relationships that his texts voice from *Catiline* onwards. The degree to which that subjection was a willing submission is a matter for biographical speculation, not criticism. In some obvious sense, that triad is a given and constitutes much of what is the "human agency" voicing itself in the text.

The work of this book is to examine the operation of the paradigm of the sexual triad in this specific text in relation to other structural features of Ibsen's play. The basic triad expands here to play itself out in a complex series of reconfigurations. Consequently, I begin my "reading" with a discussion of these transformations in the inter-relationships of the five principals as the *action* of the play. I follow this chapter with an essay that documents the processes in which the play positions this reconfiguration within a specific socioeconomic structure and an idea of economy that integrates Ibsen's liberal critique of capitalism with his representation of sexual value. With that foundation laid, I take up the question of Hedda's character and its implication in the gender issues that we find important at the end of this century. One of those issues deals with the notion of discourse, narrative, the illusion of comprehensive vision as part of male self-definition that excludes the female as the kind of subject that formulates and sustains language. I discuss the ways in which the principal narrative consciousness—the primary visionary—in the play, Eilert Løvborg, is moved to the edges of our focus because our attention is directed to Hedda Gabler who does not define her reality in narrative terms. In a separate chapter I discuss the transformation of Ibsen's usual narrative emphasis into the series of interrogations that direct the expository dialogue of this play. I conclude with a chapter that deals with what I call "The Rhetoric of Circumlocution." Hedda's class determines what can and cannot be spoken in her presence, and—isolated, if not imprisoned in the Falk Villa—she receives the data of the world filtered through the language of those who have access to it. Because of Hedda's continual presence, we have access to that world only through the circumlocutions in which its sordid details can be discussed before her. In this final chapter I discuss the implications of the indirection of language that the text holds as requisite.

5

Reconfiguration as Action

Hedda Gabler organizes itself in a series of personal and sexual relationships in which the basic triangle functions more as a momentary
point of stability in a dynamic process of desire and substitution than
as a fixed structure in which the text characterizes the three principals
of a sexual triad. These fluid triangular relationships figure in a process in which one figure desires another and accepts a substitute who
ultimately fails to meet the demands of that desire. The text posits a
series of provisional relationships—between Thea and Tesman, Hedda
and Tesman, Thea and Løvborg, Hedda and Løvborg, Hedda and
Brack—that transform themselves during its course. In this chapter, I
focus upon the processes in which *Hedda Gabler* orders this series of
relationships between different pairs of the principals before developing the final structure that focuses upon the surviving Thea and
Tesman, whose pairing reenacts the relationship of Thea and Eilert.

In the brief expository dialogue between Frøken Julle Tesman and
her former maid, Berte, we gain some sense of their social and emotional distance from the figure of Hedda Gabler, the bride of Frøken
Tesman's nephew, Jørgen. Recall that the newly married couple has
arrived the night before from their wedding journey to take up resi-

dence in the villa the scene represents. The limited discussion between the aunt and the servant who has been reassigned to the nephew's household documents their surprise that Jørgen Tesman has married this exceptional young woman and, as well, their apprehension of their own position in regard to her. In the succeeding dialogue with Tesman, Hedda's status within the town as the daughter of the late general emerges even more clearly. The potential estrangement between Frøken Tesman and the new bride is illustrated graphically by the reference to the fact that after meeting their steamer at the pier, she had to arrange her own transportation from the dock because Hedda insisted on filling the hired carriage with her luggage. As the discussion between aunt and nephew focuses upon Jørgen's present success and the assurance of his future, Frøken Tesman makes a hostile reference to his former rival: " . . . and the people who stood in your way . . . and wanted to keep you back . . . you outran them all. They've fallen by the wayside, Jørgen! And your most dangerous adversary, he fell lower than any of them, he did. . . . And now he must lie on the bed he's made for himself . . . the poor depraved creature" (178–79). In the following line, in a tone that doesn't argue with his aunt but suggests his more benevolent attitude toward his competitor and friend, Tesman identifies the "poor depraved creature" as Løvborg.

Hedda's arrival in the room itself sustains the sense of her alienation from her husband's principal relation and presents her as curiously isolated emotionally from her husband. Her language, gracious in syntax and distant in substance, seems to express a determination to hold herself apart from involvement with the Tesman family. Here, in a stage moment that has become notorious, Hedda pretends to believe that Frøken Tesman's hat, which Tesman has placed on a chair, belongs to the maid who has carelessly left it there. Hedda's pretense, of course, is not obvious at the moment, but—as in other phenomena of her behavior—she reveals her motive in a later dialogue, in this instance, with Judge Brack later in the act.

In the brief period between Hedda's discovery of the note from Thea Elvsted, née Rysing, and the woman's arrival, she playfully teases Tesman about his earlier relationship with Thea by referring to her as

Din gamle flamme (your old flame). Here the Norwegian and English idioms share the same metaphor. The brief reference in this early conversation between Hedda and Tesman places Thea in a previous relationship with Tesman—in a relationship sufficiently developed to have been discussed in a conversation that Hedda could have heard. This segment of dialogue, for a moment at least, hypothesizes a triad of Jørgen, Hedda, Thea, and suggests Hedda as a more brilliant replacement for Tesman's earlier sexual choice. While in the draft material of this section of dialogue, Tesman identifies Løvborg as Hedda's "old flame," as well, the final version suppresses our knowledge of this symmetry until its revelation in act 2. Because secrecy is an important part of the relationship between Hedda and Løvborg, as this later conversation reveals, this deferral of information and the elimination of Tesman's knowledge of it protects its privacy from public view. The secrecy allows the relationship to take the form of a series of surreptitious encounters that, if known, would be seen as transgressions of morality even if they didn't include actual physical sexuality. But to return to the early point of the play: when Hedda refers to Tesman's earlier relationship with Thea Elvsted, the spectator also knows that his history includes a former competitive relationship with Eilert Løvborg.

Consequently, by the moment of Thea Elvsted's entrance, the spectator has in mind the following alignment: (1) the relationship of Thea to Jørgen, as a former sexual interest and, therefore, directly involved in Tesman's history; (2) Thea's relationship with Hedda as a school acquaintance and a less distinct aspect of her past than of Tesman's; and, (3) Thea's potential relationship to Tesman's former rival, Løvborg, because of his proximity as an inhabitant of the remote region consistently identified in the text as *der oppe* (up there). In addition to these configurations, the expository dialogue between Tesman and Aunt Julle also suggests, obliquely, some kind of relationship between Judge Brack and Hedda. Tesman reveals that the purchase of the Falk Villa has been implemented by Brack, who was able to obtain an advantageous mortgage for Tesman, and that he conveyed this information through correspondence with Hedda, not with Tesman himself. Frøken Tesman, who confesses that she has mortgaged her annuity in order to furnish the house, reveals that Brack has also arranged "the formality" of that lien.

The dialogue among Hedda, Thea, and (in part) Tesman reveals more complex interrelationships: particularly, the alignment between Thea and Løvborg. After Tesman removes himself, responding to Hedda's manipulative suggestion that he write Løvborg a personal note of invitation, Thea moves through a series of verbal subterfuges that attempt to disguise her potentially sexual relationship to Løvborg, but she is forced by Hedda's insistent questioning to reveal critical details of her history with him. First of all, she identifies Løvborg as someone about whom she knew while she lived in town, then as her husband's friend, and her stepchildren's tutor (who replaced her in the responsibility of educating Elvsted's children). Under Hedda's keenly focused interrogation, she confesses that Eilert is more her friend than her husband's, that she has assisted in his reformation as an alcoholic and, as well, that she has worked with him—or, at least, been present—while he has written his new book. She manifests surprise and pleasure when Hedda describes their relationship as one between *to gode kamerater*—"two good comrades"—because this term is precisely the one that Eilert has used himself to characterize their relationship.[1] The dialogue between Eilert and Hedda in act 2 reveals that this term is one with which he described his former relationship with Hedda. When the later conversation offers this delayed revelation, we return, in memory, to Hedda's interrogation of Thea in the first act, revise our sense of its significance and, in retrospect, understand the energy with which she undertakes it. In rethinking the scene, we invest her question—"Like two good comrades, then?"—with the combination of irony and jealousy that we now realize must have driven it. Ibsen's suppression or deferral of the information about Hedda's relationship with Eilert Løvborg forces us to witness the controlled tension of this conversation with Thea Elvsted without understanding its motives. Our need, therefore, to return, in memory, to this scene, and to reprocess its data during the course of the second act, complicates our sense of the drama as a sequential progress. After we receive the deferred clarification of Hedda's behavior, we listen to her language and watch her gestures more carefully because we recognize that we do not have full or ready access to the motives of her action.

Immediately after this reference to her relationship with Eilert as a comradeship, Thea introduces the equivocal figure of the woman whose presence in the undisclosed narrative of the past provides an obstacle—in the words of the text, a shadow—that keeps Eilert somehow distant from her. Eilert mentioned this woman, only once, she claims, when he told her that she threatened to shoot him when they separated. Thea suggests that this woman may be the red-haired singer who, according to report, carried a loaded pistol. Again, this exchange between the two women presents information that the dialogue between Hedda and Eilert will later correct as it reveals unequivocally that the woman who threatened Eilert as well as the original "good comrade" is Hedda herself. The red-haired figure, later named as Frøken Diana by Judge Brack, becomes a convenient instrument of Hedda's own circumlocution as she reinforces Thea's misconception of the identity of the woman who dominates Løvborg's memory.

The coordinates of the relationship between Hedda and Brack become clearer in act 2. In chapter 9 I discuss the conversations between Hedda and Brack in this act in some detail as I analyze their uses of circumlocution. Here, however, I focus on the sequence in which Ibsen's text patterns the relationship between Hedda and this older friend from her circle. As she discusses the fact that Tesman was the only one of her admirers willing to provide for her, she *"banteringly"* claims that she expected no offer for marriage from Brack himself. In the second part of her conversation with Brack in act 2, Hedda alludes to her relationship with Brack by outlining the general circumstances that led to her relationship with Tesman.

HEDDA: . . . I used Tesman as an escort to take me home from evening parties last summer. . . .

BRACK: Ah, regrettably . . . I had to go quite a different way.

HEDDA: True enough, you were going a rather different way, last summer. (210–11)

Now, apparently unsatisfied with that relationship, Brack attempts to maneuver Hedda into becoming a sexual partner. He subtly suggests the formation of a triangular relationship in which he may come and go at will as a "trusted friend . . . Candidly of the lady." The alert spectator recognizes, of course, that the triangular relationship that Brack proposes would replicate the situation at the Elvsted home that Thea reports, under pressure, to Hedda: a wife, dissatisfied and bored with her husband, shifts her attention, and eventually her emotional loyalty, to the regular visitor whose conversation enlivens her otherwise-restricted life. Brack's relationship with Hedda will also duplicate her earlier relationship with Eilert, as he tries unsuccessfully to shift his relationship with her from one realized primarily in language to one consummated physically. At this point, of course, we do not have the information to see that specific correspondence. When we do learn about Løvborg's attempt to transform a relationship embodied in language to one realized through sex, we can identify the Brack strategy as a repetition, in some sense, of an earlier event in the narrative history of the play. At this point, we witness the relationship between Hedda and Brack only in contrast to her relationship with Tesman. We do identify, of course, an erotic charge underneath the subtle aggressiveness of their dialogue that radically differentiates their interaction from that between Hedda and her husband.

Hedda's pleasure in Brack's company focuses upon his skill as a "conversationalist," in contrast to the boring recitations of the "specialist." Hedda neither acquiesces to Brack nor unequivocally refuses him until he attempts to extort his sexual privilege by blackmailing her at the end of the drama. Hedda's emphasis upon conversation here is not merely a strategy of circumlocution. And yet, as in her reference to the "two good comrades" in the first act, we have no idea of the erotic implications of her image of conversation. Before Eilert's reappearance, Judge Brack offers himself to Hedda, and she, undoubtedly, thinks of him as a substitute for Eilert, as someone with whom she can talk—even within the bounds of her marriage to the specialist. At this point, however, we remain unclear as to the significance that each of these skillful rhetoricians attaches to the term *conversation*.

Reconfiguration as Action

By the end of the dialogue between Eilert and Hedda in the second act, we have a fuller sense of a series of alignments among six characters: Hedda, Tesman, Thea, Brack, Løvborg, and the red-haired woman later named by Brack as Frøken Diana. In a subtle verbal economy, the text outlines a tentative narrative that builds on a series of substitutions or exchanges among these six. The performance itself displays that unelaborated narrative simultaneously with the representation of the present action. As the structure of this chapter attempts to clarify, the interrelationships among these figures is dynamic, and we process the present and past alignments simultaneously with our recognition of the present configuration. However, the language of the play does not reveal the past as cohesive history but, rather, as partially articulated segments of information that the characters reveal to each other in an effort to conceal as much as reveal.

For example, the image of the past relationship between Hedda and Eilert that evolves in their dialogue describes a series of hidden conversations in the presence of General Gabler and a relationship known only to themselves. Even though this description puts forward the most detailed reconstitution of the past in this text, it offers a very shadowy picture of a wordly, sensual young man who is encouraged by a young woman to speak of his erotic exploits and, as well, to limit their relationship to that conversation. The dialogue in which that information is revealed models the conversations it reports by enacting a polite but distant review of photographs, partially overheard by Brack and Tesman, and by being actually a reminiscence of their earlier relationship. Because of the present nature of their relationship and the situation of their conversation, however, that dialogue suppresses more data than it reveals.

Hedda's actual sexual experience, limited to her marriage with Tesman, has had less of an impact on her than have these surreptitious erotic conversations with Eilert some years earlier. Acutely afraid of society's condemnation of sexual transgressions, Hedda's sexual behavior has been restrained, except in the oblique language of these meetings. Consequently, the potential excitement of the frequent appearance of Brack, in private visits with her, carries an erotic charge that continues her displacement of sexuality into an exchange of words. After hearing of Hedda's conversations with Løvborg and Hedda's sense of their significance, Brack's use of the image of conversation, extending the use of conversation in both a literal and a metaphoric sense, aligns perfectly with Hedda's previous experience of displacing sexuality into dialogue or interrogation. Hedda's sexual repression—manifesting her appropriation of society's condemnation—forces her to make this substitution of language for sex. Even within that substitution, the reality of sexuality must limit its form of expression to the indirection of circumlocution.

Whereas the text alludes to this relationship between the dissolute younger Løvborg and the boldly curious younger Hedda Gabler only briefly and without precise description, the *comradeship* of that sequence of interrogations and confessions becomes the dominant model of relationship for both dramatic figures. In this paradigm, language—dialogue, interrogation, confession—substitutes for sexual action. In terms of the pattern of one character's dependence upon another, Hedda's use of Eilert Løvborg to gain access to a world denied her contributes to the intricate interlocking relationship of the principal characters of this drama. In that sense, Eilert functions as a substitute for Hedda herself in her imagination, a surrogate figure through whom she can experience the world. Løvborg's relationship with the younger Hedda is covertly sexual and exists only as language in their practice of allowing her to interrogate him about his life outside the bounds of society. Hedda's model of sexual freedom, therefore, figures itself in a male image. Her use of the Nietzschean figure of the Dionysian with vine leaves in his hair projects this vision of the romantic bacchanal upon the alcoholic excesses of the young man. His reformation, of course, despoils him in Hedda's eyes because that imposed morality restrains the very excess that formed the basis of their relationship and her imagined access to the world. This bourgeois despoiling stimulates her to retrieve the previous Løvborg, and she sets out to provide him with the temptation that will force him to resume his previous behavior. We perceive the details of that behavior, of course, in allusive but unspecific references.

Reconfiguration as Action

In performance, the partially exposed past contextualizes the present but never provides sufficient clarity to give the audience a comprehensive vision of the history of these characters. We have access to the narrative of the past only through the highly self-conscious language of the characters whose verbal strategies operate to censor their revelations to the other characters as much as to inform them. The resulting narrative structure and configuration of characters develops, therefore, as a rather spare model of exchanges whose substance remains undisplayed. For example, the *re*constructed narrative that develops through the course of performance begins with two basic pairs: Hedda and Løvborg, Thea and Tesman. At the point of the dramatized moment, these couples have reconfigured themselves with the exchange of Løvborg and Tesman; however, an intermediate figure stands in the middle of each exchange. Between her relationships with Løvborg and Tesman, Hedda has been involved with Brack, who did not marry her; and Thea has become the partner, or potential partner, of Løvborg only after her unsatisfactory marriage of convenience with her employer, Elvsted. And, as I've noted earlier, the play ends with the potentiality of a return to one half of the original configuration: the pairing of Thea and Tesman. However, this return represents, in some sense, another substitution since this cooperative relationship partially, at least, reenacts the collaboration between Thea and Løvborg. As they form a relationship as *to gode kamerater* (two good comrades) to reconstruct the destroyed manuscript, ironically Thea and Tesman reembody the relationship between Thea and Eilert which itself may have been for Eilert a reenactment and substitution of his lost relationship with Hedda.

Ibsen's text isolates the five principal figures—Hedda, Tesman, Thea, Løvborg, and Brack—and the absent Diana by removing them from both parents and children. Hedda has no parents; Tesman is an orphan raised by his aunts; Løvborg is estranged from his family; Brack is childless and unmarried; Thea is childless, estranged from her husband, and sufficiently distanced emotionally from her stepchildren that she never actually names them in her single conversational reference to them. Thea's comment that she never had a home of her own

51

makes no reference to her childhood, and the fact that she stays in some kind of temporary lodgings suggests that she has no close relatives remaining in the town where she was educated. The text of this play makes no statement concerning General Gabler's death and offers no explanations for Hedda's lack of financial resources. There is no reference to the death of Hedda's mother, and the few references to the general suggest a rather extended period in which there was only General Gabler and his daughter. In the draft material, Hedda does not refer to a mother and in conversation with Brack notes that she was "the child of an old man—and a worn-out man too—or past his prime at any rate."[2] Frøken Julle names Tesman's dead father, Jochum, and marks Jørgen's aptitude for organizing collections and documents as related to his father's abilities. She provides no information about his parents' death. One consequence of this combination of familial isolation and estrangement is the intensity of the focus upon the internal dynamics of this group and its reconfiguration during the course of the play. Another consequence relates to my later discussion of suppressed exposition, the practice in which Ibsen ellides any narrative reference that does not inform the immediate dramatized action. A third consequence of this concentration upon the present generation is the emphasis gained in the comparison between the two *children*, the fetus Hedda carries and the symbolic child of Eilert's manuscript.

The text suggests that during the period of Eilert Løvborg's earlier relationship with Hedda he maintained a sexual relationship with Frøken Diana, whom Brack describes as a singer, "as well." With the subtle allusiveness of this phrase, Brack identifies Diana as a prostitute without using the offensive *noun* in Hedda's presence. In the time immediately preceding the dramatic action, Løvborg depends upon Thea, but distances himself because of the memory of the unnamed woman the text later identifies as Hedda. Recall that Hedda allows Thea to think that this unidentified woman is the red-haired Diana. The identification of Løvborg's connection to Frøken Diana also suggests that she may be the object of his earlier misadventures. When he attempted to shift his relationship with the general's daughter into an overtly sexual one, Hedda threatened to shoot him and then renounced him. In other words, in this incident, Løvborg attempts to coerce Hedda to become an active participant in the adventures that his confessions to her describe and, in that sense, to become a substitute for one of those partners, perhaps a substitute for the role played by Diana herself. However, in that moment in the narrative past of the play, Eilert Løvborg acts out his experience within a structure that differentiates the sexual relationship with Diana from the "intimate and confidential" relationship with Hedda. In this reconstructed narrative, therefore, we can see that Diana and Hedda constitute different but related objects of Løvborg's sexual desire and clearly function as substitutes for each other.

The unseen Diana constitutes an intriguing technical device in Ibsen's play. In the first place, she provides a kind of screen upon which individual characters can project images of life outside the limits of acceptable social behavior. As we have seen, Hedda uses Thea's knowledge of Diana's implication in Løvborg's history to deflect the possibility that Thea would identify her as the principal female in Eilert's past. Brack later uses Hedda's knowledge of Diana's prostitution to substantiate the social unacceptability of Eilert's behavior. Later, as well, he exploits that knowledge to destroy Hedda's idealization of the writer's death. Diana's overt sexuality and her availability as a sexual partner make her a physical substitute in answering Eilert's sexual desire, initially for Hedda, and—during the moment dramatized—perhaps his desire for both Hedda and Thea. His desire for Thea may be a redirection of his desire for Hedda, and his present sexual relationship with Diana, a process of subsituting Diana for Thea, who substitutes for the original Hedda. Curiously, in Hedda's final moment—her unseen behavior in the backroom—she aligns herself with Diana. The text identifies the music she plays as a *dansemelodi*, not a selection from Schumann or Chopin, but the kind of "lively" popular music that would be played at Diana's. As Hedda plays the offensive music behind the closed draperies, irritating both Thea and Tesman, she momentarily turns the Falk Villa from the restrained site of mourning to the self-consciously energetic ambiance of Diana's quarters.

Frøken Diana, as well, may have been the stimulus that forced

Brack "to go quite a different way" and, through his unavailability, indirectly provide the occasion for Hedda's relationship with Tesman to develop. While the text represents the events of this particular narrative in subtle, unverifiable suggestions, it is not outside of the mode of the text to speculate on the involvement of the red-haired singer in the stories of both Eilert and Brack. This speculation provides the opportunity to enclose the implicit narrative in a perfectly symmetrical dynamic. The text names no other woman, and it seems appropriate to the economy of this drama to identify Diana as the figure whose presence completes the structure of the three sexual couples whose configuration and reconfiguration comprise the action of the play. If we identify Frøken Diana as the woman who led Brack away from Hedda Gabler the summer before, we can extrapolate another triad: Brack, Hedda, and Diana. In the draft material, the judge confesses to Hedda that he never suspected that the engagement with Tesman would lead anywhere; and he agrees with her that "The wish was father to the thought."[3] As in the final script, Hedda tells Brack that she held no expectations that the judge himself would marry her. Later, in this material, she alludes to Brack's withdrawal of his attention to her in favor of one of the "young married ladies," a withdrawal that occasioned her use of Tesman as an escort home. In the finished version, Hedda simply identifies Brack's defection, and he agrees that he "needed to go in an entirely different direction." Ibsen's deletion of the reference to a "younger" lady, ostensibly of their circle, opens the possibility that the direction Brack traveled may have been toward Diana. His later reference to her physical strength suggests direct knowledge of the woman. While the text certainly does not identify the triad of Brack, Hedda, and Diana—with Diana constituting a sexual substitute for the unavailable Hedda—the occlusion of specific references opens up that possibility.

Henrik Ibsen's *Hedda Gabler* suggests a world external to the drawing room of the villa that comprises the theatrical scene of this play. Hedda and Tesman have just returned from an extended European journey, and all of the characters except Hedda move into the immediate world of this city, which may specifically represent Oslo.

But the world outside of this scene remains inaccessible to the spectator. While Brack and Hedda make reference to the circle that comprises their social set, these persons remain absent from the city during the time frame of this play. The world of the play is not limited to Hedda, Brack, Tesman, Thea, Løvborg, Frøken Julle, and Berte. Three significant named figures play important roles: Elvsted, Rina Tesman (Julle's invalid and dying sister), and Frøken Diana. The guests at Brack's party and the police extend the world of the play. But the principal—even the exclusive—focus of this text remains on the reconfiguration, the exchanging of roles among the six sexual figures of the play: the five principals and the unseen Diana. The absence of Diana, as physical presence, remains consistent with the practice in *Hedda Gabler* of appropriating only those aspects of the world that can be discussed within the linguistic boundaries imposed in the drawing room of the Falk Villa. Frøken Diana could never be present in this space, and her specific identity—as prostitute and companion to Eilert and, ostensibly, Brack—can be alluded to only obliquely. Consequently, this key figure in the plot of the drama exists only in critical but necessarily indirect reference. The fact that Diana enters Ibsen's composition of the play late in its writing suggests that he uses this unseen figure as a connecting tissue to complete the symmetry of a structure already in place.

The action of *Hedda Gabler* is a perverse dance among these six participants. The most vital couple destroy themselves and leave the remaining four with partners who function as substitutes for those who have died. Hedda and Eilert form the center of that sextet, and the others, in varying degrees of attenuation, function momentarily as their substitutes but ultimately fail to reify the originals. Even before the play resolves itself with Hedda's suicide, Thea and Jørgen are set up as an inadequate re-embodiment of the relationship of Thea and Eilert; with Hedda's death, that imitative relationship may remain intact. Hedda and Eilert—as the principals—embody idealized objects of desire for the others. Both Thea and Diana function as substitutes for the unavailable Hedda. Eilert provides the male counterpart of Hedda's brilliant attraction, and his vitality and vision make him the most energetic and energizing male figure, whose perceived value defines the inadequacy of the other males, especially for Hedda.

Ibsen's realistic texts almost invariably invest their domestic interiors with a kind of historical sequence in the minds of their characters. The complicated series of rooms in the Ekdal flat includes the garret that holds the artificially created replica of the woods at Hoidal and functions as a refuge that accepts the characters' evasion of reality. Eventually, of course, it is transformed into the "bottom of the sea" in Hedvig's suicidal development of that metaphor. The rooms of *A Doll's House,* furnished in the exacting taste of Torvald Helmer, contain, but do not express, the sensibility of Nora. The portraits of army and clergy coincide with the oppressive Rosmer inheritance in Johannes's consciousness to form *Rosmersholm* as both physical site and state of mind. The rooms where Halvard Solness work and live represent his personal efforts to structure reality; and the horizontally divided house of *John Gabriel Borkman* both encloses a dense and complicated family history and offers itself as a visual representation of that history.

While Hedda sustains the untruth that the Falk Villa is the home she has desired, she asserts her dislike for this house and her estrangement from it to Brack in what we can interpret as a rare honest statement. She returns to a home furnished by another, and identifies very little with it. Tesman, enthusiastic as its owner, remains, in his fundamentally bourgeois sensibility, out of place in this spacious and elegant, if old-fashioned, environment. Brack, Løvborg, and Thea come into this space as visitors. Consequently, in an important sense, each of these figures—caught in the machine of events that Ibsen appropriates from the *pièce bien faite*—is also trapped in an unfamiliar place and forced to play out the complications of this drama in a site that holds no extended history for them. Only a few objects have been brought from the Gabler home, a site invoked only in the memory of Hedda's and Eilert's afternoon conversations. The piano, the portrait of the general, the pistols in their case—these objects temporarily positioned in the villa call attention to the fact that this space and most of the objects contained within it sustain no emotional resonance for these characters. In that sense, Ibsen isolates his configuration of characters in a curious atemporality. The action plays itself out in a space peculiarly neutralized, overseen by the imposing portrait of General Gabler, about whom we know virtually nothing. The past, as always in Ibsen, voices itself in *Hedda Gabler,* but here that crucial history most often speaks slightly out of range of our hearing. Consequently, our attention remains sharply focused on the dynamics of the present and the intricacies with which this configuration of dramatic figures works toward its final structure. In a sense, all of these principals are on equal ground here, even though Hedda's persuasive claim for attention may keep them from recognizing it. The dominant image of the general's portrait commanding attention in this house—unfamiliar to its inhabitants and those who visit them—reminds us that the painting and the heroine have been displaced. We learn that this residence has been purchased on a mortgage, arranged by Judge Brack, on the intangible collateral of Tesman's pending university appointment. Ibsen's text displays the dynamic of reconfiguration within the terms of an economy in which each of these principals, except Brack, lives at risk. The drawing room of the Falk Villa, tentatively held in Tesman's precarious situation, is both the scene and the emblem of that risk.

6

Social Structure

Ibsen's *Hedda Gabler* belongs to both the realistic mode of playwriting that brought Ibsen popular fame and the antirealistic mode that would soon take over the avant-garde. At the same time in which the literal surface of the later plays attempts to encapsulate the visual and behavioral appearance of the spectator's world, the experiences of their protagonists deny the possibility of sustaining a comprehensive vision of reality. Solness, Rosmer, Allmers, Borkman, and Rubek embody the skeptical recognition that they cannot write a discourse or create a physical artifact that represents reality in any form other than a false stabilization of its inherent dynamics. As well, these texts point toward their own artificiality in a delicately wrought process of self-referentiality that clarifies their formal quality.

Hedda Gabler "pretends" to point toward a socioeconomic segment of Norwegian society in the 1890s as its "particular referent." I emphasize the verb "pretend" in the sense that Terry Eagleton uses it in his discussion of the relationship between fiction and reality in realist literature. In *Criticism and Ideology,* Eagleton distinguishes between the obvious artificiality of the "poetic" statement and the illusory authenticity of the realist text. The "poetic" text clarifies the distance between the signifier and the signified whereas the realist text pretends to unify the form of the statement and its referent:

> Both statements in fact belong to literary discourses which lack a real particular referent; it is simply that in the first case this absence inscribes itself in the very letter of the text, which proclaims its lack of a real object in its very internal disproportionment of elements, flaunts its relative autonomy of the real in the formal structures of its proposition. It is the very eloquence of the "poetic" which alludes to a kind of silence. Realist prose, on the other hand, "pretends" to a real particular referent in its every phrase, only to unmask that pretence in its status as a complete discourse ["novel"]. The "poetic" is in this sense its concealed truth, parading in its very microstructures the macrostructural character of the realist work.[1]

Eagleton asserts that realist works of fiction project the illusion that a specific objective world is their referent but that "The literary text's lack of a real direct referent constitutes the most salient fact about it: its fictiveness."[2] In realist works, according to Eagleton, the "poetic" constitutes its concealed hidden structure that points toward the actual signified. The literal surface of the realist work points toward a referent that is virtual, not actual. In chapter 4, I discuss Michael Fried's use of the terms *graphic* and *pictorial*. That aspect of Ibsen's text that "pretends" to hold a particular referent corresponds to its graphic function. Our awareness of the aesthetic construct, partially concealed by the illusion of the literal, forces us to see the artistically forced structure of the text as its submission to a structure that directs it.

In chapter 4, for example, I point to the relationship of Hjørdis and Sigurd, Dagny and Gunnar in *The Vikings at Helgeland* as prototypical of the relationship among the four principals of *Hedda Gabler* despite the fact that each drama appears to refer to a radically different historical moment and implements a distinctive theatrical form of its own. We need to recognize that the specific socioeconomic structure that appears in *Hedda Gabler* is not the object—or, in Eagleton's term—the referent of its process of representation. That recognition, of course, should not stimulate us, however, to ignore the details of that illusion of a literal truthfulness to the coordinates of the socioeconomic structure of Oslo in 1890 or slightly earlier. We should look at that virtual literalness, not as structure to which Ibsen's text conforms in the subordination of art to socioeconomic reality, but as the vehicle, the agency, the instrument through which his writing works out its own highly individual structure.

In *Hedda Gabler* the risk of poverty threatens each of the characters except Judge Brack. For reasons that the playwright refused to make accessible, General Gabler's death has left Hedda without any substantive financial resources, and the sole legacy of this man seems to be his portrait and his dueling pistols. Consequently, Hedda—at twenty-nine, late in the competition for marriage—depends upon a husband for financial security. Thea, whose situation forced her to accept employment as a governess, also married for security and is dependent upon her husband. Leaving Elvsted to follow Eilert Løvborg, Thea puts herself at risk. Løvborg's abandonment of her leaves her unprotected economically and socially. Both Hedda and Thea have used their own sexuality to gain husbands to support them; and their use of marriage represents a socially legitimate means of subsistence. The image of Diana, whose career as a professional singer encompasses prostitution, represents the illegitimate, socially unacceptable uses of sexuality for economic survival. In the notes to the play, however, Ibsen provides his provisional version of Hedda with a clear-eyed recognition of the parallels between her situation and that of this woman whose life is outside the social world of the play: "isn't it an honourable thing to profit by one's person? Don't actresses and others turn their advantages into profit? I had no other capital. Marriage—I thought it was like buying an annuity."[3]

Tesman, who uses Brack to arrange the purchase of the home he wishes to provide Hedda, assumes a large debt on the basis of his prospective appointment as professor. In order to furnish this home, his Aunt Julle, Frøken Tesman, risks the capital that provides the small income that supports her and her invalid sister. Eilert Løvborg, who, unlike Tesman, comes from an "influential" family, has spent his inheritance and, therefore, like Tesman is financially dependent upon his work as a scholar. He declares shortly after his arrival at the Tesman villa that he has written a book that will please the public as the first step of reestablishing himself. At the moment of the play itself, he has the money generated by this recently published book; but as Tesman clarifies, this payment is not enough to live on. That income does give him the freedom to return, temporarily, to the way of life that depleted his inheritance. The text aligns Løvborg's inclination for dissolute behavior and his economic status. His more controlled life, under Thea's influence, is facilitated by his lack of funds; and when he gets money from the sale of his book, it is easier for him to succumb to temptation. Eilert exhausts his financial, psychic, and intellectual resources simultaneously so that, at the end of the drama, he has nothing for him, or for Thea, to live on, either economically or emotionally.

Hedda Gabler, the daughter of a general, has the social background, the experience, expectations, taste, and appetite for a life that her economic status can no longer bring her. Tesman, whose background is closer to the center of the middle class, has come into contact with her circle, probably through his success as a student, perhaps his friendship with Eilert Løvborg, and his recognized potential to become a distinguished professor. However, the early conversation between Frøken Tesman and Berte clarifies that the Tesmans live outside of the circle Hedda defines as so important to her. When Tesman faces the hard facts of his debt and the problems with his appointment, he declares to Brack that he could not put Hedda into a bourgeois setting. The implication is, of course, that the Tesman household, the rooms he shared with his aunts, is precisely the kind of middle class environment that Hedda would abhor. At no point does the text include a suggestion that Hedda would even visit the home of the Tesman aunts. The informal contractual basis of her marriage with Tesman, as the dialogue at the end of act 1 details, asserts that he will provide her with a house that will become the arena for her life within society. When they discuss the financial limitations imposed by the deferral of his appointment, Hedda reminds him of this verbal contract:

HEDDA: [*rising slowly and tiredly*] The agreement was that we were to live a social life. Entertain.

TESMAN: Yes, oh Heavens . . . I was so looking foreward to it! Just think, to see you as the hostess . . . presiding over a select group of friends! Eh? . . . Well, well, well, for the time being we'll just have to be the two of us, Hedda. Just see Aunt Julle once in a while . . . Oh, for you everything should have been so very . . . very different . . . !

HEDDA: And I suppose I won't get my footman just yet awhile. (201)

Commentary on *Hedda Gabler* often claims that Hedda's aesthetic sensibility distances her from Tesman's more mundane temperament. I have read critics, for example, who cite Hedda's disinterest in Tesman's slippers, embroidered by Frøken Rina and her unwillingness to visit the dying invalid as evidence of her artistic sense. Consider, however, the ways in which the language of the play marks what this dramatic figure values and what she rejects: Hedda responds negatively to the abundance of flowers in the drawing room; she voices her disinterest in Tesman's slippers; she notes, without value, the dry, yellow leaves outside of the French doors; she marks the inappropriateness of her old piano in the room furnished by Frøken Julle and Brack; she professes interest in the sporting aspect of the competition between Løvborg and Tesman; she displays clear disinterest in the intellectual content of Løvborg's book and the unpublished manuscript and conceptualizes it only as a symbol of his relationship with Thea; she develops an image of suicide as "beautiful," equating the heroism and aestheticism of this act. The only time we hear her play the piano is when she plays the inappropriately timed *dansemelodi* shortly before her suicide. At no point does she refer to art, literature, or music. She makes no aesthetic references to the places she and Tesman visited on their recent journey, and—significantly—she does not characterize the limitations of Tesman, the specialist, by marking the differences in their responses to the art and architecture they encountered during this journey. The play presents no concrete evidence of Hedda's aesthetic or intellectual interests, and the distance that Hedda perceives between herself and the social environment of the Tesman family that attempts to enclose her is not based on her greater aesthetic sense but, rather, on her sense of class difference. When Tesman asks her to visit the dying Rina, she responds, "No, no don't ask me. I don't want to look at sickness and death. I must be free of everything that's ugly" (239). Hedda's artistic sensitivity does not energize her refusal; when the moment comes to build an image of Eilert's death and, eventually, her own, as an aesthetic construct in her imagination, she does not view death as *ugly*. She distances herself from Frøken Rina's deathbed because she is unwilling to be drawn into the degrading reality of Tesman's bourgeois family drama.

The dramatis personae of *Hedda Gabler* display the class structure of western Europe at the end of the nineteenth century. The text carefully differentiates Hedda, Judge Brack, and Eilert Løvborg—as representatives of the haute bourgeoisie—from the other figures in the drama. The conversations between Brack and Hedda reveal that they share a social circle (whose members we learn are still abroad into September) that is outside of the experience of those with whom Tesman's academic work will bring them into contact. Eilert Løvborg, unlike Jørgen Tesman, seems to have been a member of that circle—at least we know he was frequently received in General Gabler's home. The language of Thea Elvsted, Jørgen Tesman, and Frøken Julle establishes their basically bourgeois position and attitude. The Tesmans' fond inclusion of the lower-class Berte in the affairs of the family marks one aspect of their middle-class sensibility. Hedda's detached reference to Berte as "the servant" voices her class-determined perception of the domestic employee as a functional anonymous adjunct to the household. She ignores the woman's presence as an individuated person, and Jørgen's familiar attitude toward Berte contributes to Hedda's recognition of her inability to fit within the middle-class structure of her marriage. When, to mask the primary motive of her destruction of Løvborg's manuscript, Hedda claims to have acted to protect Tesman, she also suggests, in the boldest manner she can, that she may be pregnant. She reacts to Tesman's exhuberant and loud response by attempting to quiet him so that Berte will not overhear:

TESMAN: [*exclaiming, torn between doubt and happiness*] Hedda, . . . oh gracious . . . is this really true! . . . Yes, but . . . yes, but . . . I never knew you loved me like that, Hedda, not in that way. Think of that!

HEDDA: Well, then I suppose I'd better tell you that . . . that just at this time . . . [*Breaks off passionately.*] Oh, no, no, you can go and ask your Auntie Julle. She'll tell you all about it.

TESMAN: Oh, I almost think I know what it is, Hedda! [*Claps his hands together.*] Oh, good heavens . . . is it really possible? Eh?

HEDDA: Don't shout like that. The maid can hear you.

TESMAN: [*laughing in the excess of his joy*] The maid: Oh, Hedda, you are really priceless. The maid, . . . why that's Berte! I'll go out and tell Berte myself.

HEDDA: [*clenches her hands as though in desperation*] Oh, it'll kill me . . . it'll kill me, all this!

TESMAN: All what, Hedda? Eh?

HEDDA: [*coldly, in control again*] All this . . . farce . . . Jørgen.

TESMAN: Farce! But it's just that I'm so happy. . . . Well, perhaps I'd better not tell Berte, then.

HEDDA: Oh yes . . . why not do the thing properly? (255)

The Norwegian term *løyerlig* (literally: drollery, comedy, peculiarity) that Jens Arup, the translator of the Oxford edition of this play, has translated as *farce* is often translated as *absurdity*.[4] *Farce* avoids its contemporary association with the *absurd* as a genre of postwar existential drama, and it is appropriate to express Hedda's disgust with her domestic situation through a term that associates Tesman's behavior with a popular comic theatrical form that Hedda would view as debased. Hedda sees herself, at this point, trapped within the family concerns with what she regards as insignificant, mundane, demeaning; and her feeling of being enmeshed in the domestic plots of this petty, bourgeois environment is based, principally, upon her awareness of the differences between classes. At this moment, the focus of her attention is, of course, on the unborn child she carries. This desperate response to Tesman's ebullient desire to make her condition public documents her desperate realization that the Tesmans will soon appropriate her pregnancy into their cloying domestic middle-class comedy.

Both Hedda and Eilert Løvborg have lost the privileges of their position in the haute bourgeoisie. Eilert has become a social pariah, estranged from his family because of the behavior that made him unacceptable to society, and Hedda—because of her lack of financial resources—solved her economic and social crisis by marrying outside of her class. And, once again, as Tesman faces the deferral or loss of his appointment, she confronts her own economic threat—even though she voices her attempt to distance herself from the circumstances of that event. In the draft material for *Hedda*, Ibsen positions Hedda more clearly outside the parameters of society by marking her father's disgrace: "Hedda speaks of how she felt herself set aside, step by step, when her father was no longer in favour, when he retired and died without leaving her anything.—It then came upon her, in her bitterness, that it was for his sake she had been made much of.—And then she was already between 25 and 26. In danger of becoming an old maid."[5] Ibsen eliminates the specificity of Hedda's fragile social status in the final draft and limits her motive for marrying Tesman to the economic crisis she confronts. Hedda asserts that she had reached a point when any acceptable marriage was necessary to survive, and she succinctly confesses her desperation to Brack: "I'd really danced myself tired, my dear sir . . . [*She gives a little shudder*]. Oh no, I'm not going to say that. Nor think it either" (206). In the earlier text Hedda's obsessive concern with the perception of society—"if only we could be free of—of what people think"—aligns with her direct experience of the social ostracism that was the consequence of Gabler's disgrace. At this point in the earlier text, Løvborg, Thea, and Hedda are discussing the need to keep the actual motive of Thea's departure from Elvsted's household a secret. Hedda internalizes that need to hide the true "connection" between Thea and Løvborg into her own desire to be able to act out her own desires, free of the constraint of her dependence upon public approval or, at least, the absence of public disapproval. She realizes that she, unlike Thea, cannot risk the social rejection such freedom would generate.

Hedda's awareness of the gaze of the public, her acute need to sustain herself as Hedda Gabler, differentiates the general's daughter from Thea. While the language of their initial dialogue suggests that Hedda responds in some awe to the bravery of Thea's action—"I don't know how you dared!" (193)—we realize that Thea's risk of social disapproval is less than Hedda's would be. That is, because Hedda is such an object of public interest—such a personage within this city— she has more to lose than Thea does. The revised text, in which Hedda's social position is not damaged by her father's disgrace, maintains her social position, a position put at risk only by her lack of financial resources and continued spinsterhood. Whereas we cannot know Ibsen's motive in removing the data concerning the general's disgrace, the result of that deletion reinforces Hedda's position within the community and focuses her problematic status on the economic issue rather than on her social status as the daughter of a disgraced public figure.

Ibsen's text organizes itself through the strategy of a series of contrasts: the differentiation of Hedda from Thea and the clarification of the differences between Eilert Løvborg and Jørgen Tesman. Their antithetical attitudes toward Eilert Løvborg's behavior reflect the class differences that divide Hedda and Thea. Errol Durbach describes Thea Elvsted as "prosaically middle-class." He continues: "[Her] major achievement has been to convert the Bohemian into a respectable and abstinent academic, stifling his vitality in the process."[6] Hedda, on the other hand, perceives Løvborg's adoption of Thea's values as a narrow-minded limitation of his engagement in life that, ironically, corrupts her idealized image of his Dionysian freedom. She perceives him as a peer within her circle who has been able to flaunt the values of society. When Hedda and Tesman speak initially about Løvborg's behavior at Brack's party, Tesman comments that "with all his talents . . . unfortunately he's quite beyond hope of reform, all the same." Hedda, still attempting to maintain her idealized vision of Eilert's freedom from the rules of behavior that seem important to her husband, focuses on Løvborg's courage to reject convention:

HEDDA: I suppose you mean he's got more courage than the rest?

TESMAN: No, good Lord . . . he just can't keep himself under control at all, you know. (236)

Ibsen's text marks a subtle difference between the attitudes of the haute bourgeoisie and the bourgeoisie. Thea, Tesman, and Frøken Julle demand an absolute integrity between morality and behavior. The class values of Hedda and Brack require the appearance of morality but tolerate what the middle class would label immorality as long as the veneer of respectability remains unmarred. Brack's life clearly involves sexual liaisons both within his class and possibly with the prostitute Diana—at least he knows that "she's a very strongly built girl, this same Miss Diana."[7] Hedda responds to his subtle and indirect references to this behavior not on the basis of its immorality, but, rather, she distances herself from its implications only in terms of his potential exercise of power over her.

The text, as I mentioned above, builds a sense of class difference, as well, between Eilert Løvborg and Jørgen Tesman. In the early dialogue between Frøken Tesman and Jørgen, the aunt celebrates the triumph of the orphaned nephew whom she has raised. Recall that her language builds an image of someone from the underclass, with implicit resentment toward the privileged. While Tesman perceives Løvborg as a friend, clearly in the Tesman household at large, this figure—handsome, bright, well-positioned in a rich and influential family—has functioned as a kind of mark against which to judge Jørgen's success and a figure whose advantages would provide the rationalization for Tesman's possible failure.

The difference between Løvborg's and Tesman's research suggests class difference as well. Løvborg's visionary method of writing history contrasts acutely with Tesman's narrow speciality on the domestic industries of Brabant in the Middle Ages. The text reveals Løvborg at the culmination of a theoretical project and Tesman at the beginning of a narrowly defined, highly limited research project. Tesman's work, and his sense of history, is tied to archival material and the collection of actual artifacts; and he perceives his work in terms of collecting and cataloging. The difference between Tesman's being enmeshed in the concrete objects of the medieval laborer's production aligns him with the work of creating these objects. He is drawn to the detritus of what Hegel would describe as the bondsman's labor. In some sense, he becomes virtually subordinate to these objects in his capacity of sorting, cataloging, and describing them. He is caught within the material circumstance of his professional work and does not see beyond those circumstances. Løvborg's archaeology is of the mind, not the artifacts of labor. The text associates Tesman's talent for organizing objects and data with his father. In that sense, his limited talent, subordinating his imagination to the rigorous and tedious minutia of research rather than the inclusive generalization of an imaginative historiography, reflects the focus of his class upon the implicit value of work and the objects it produces. Løvborg's greater vision—and his disinterest in the kind of empirical research that marks Tesman's work—reflects the greater freedom of his class from the material circumstances of production and the opportunity for reflection.

The play reveals an indirect but clear relationship between social class and sexual attractiveness. Within the group of the five sexual characters physically present in this dramatic work, Hedda and Eilert constitute the most desired figures of their sex; and the base of that attraction derives from their physical beauty, their energy, and, as well, from a distinction that is based, at least partially, on their social class. From the perspective of the bourgeois Frøken Tesman, Jørgen Tesman, and the lower-class Berte, Hedda's exceptional nature derives, at least in part, from her distance from their world. She is the beautiful general's daughter who rode with her father through the streets of the city, dressed in a black riding habit. Løvborg's alienation from the social world is more graphic because of the fact that, at one time, he commanded respect both because of intellectual distinction and his social standing as the hope of an "influential" and prosperous family. Both aspects of that distinction inform Frøken Julle's sense of the threat he posed the more bourgeois Tesman. Tesman's relationship with Hedda and Thea's relationship with Eilert seem miraculous to them because of the social improbability of these misalliances. In the expository dialogue between Tesman and Frøken Julle, they exchange their mutual surprise that Tesman won the distinguished Hedda Gabler: "Well just think of it, so now you're a married man, Jørgen! . . . And to think that you'd be the one to walk off with Hedda Gabler! The lovely Hedda Gabler! Imagine it! So many admirers she always had around her!" (175). Tesman responds by speculating on the envy his prize has generated among his friends. Hedda's relationship with Tesman has become possible because of her economic disenfranchisement, and the social estrangement and economic failure caused by Eilert's sexual and alcoholic excess makes him available to Thea. Significantly, while both Hedda and Løvborg have, in the past, enjoyed the attention and interest of their world as exceptional creatures, circumstances have compromised their value and each has reduced expectations.

Despite the fact that Thea and Hedda live in two different social circles, both marry because of economic necessity, as I've noted. Both of these marriages of convenience are threatened by the perceived eroticism of Eilert Løvborg, whose presence stimulates the women to behave outside of convention: Thea leaves her home and Hedda provides Eilert with the physical means to kill himself, the pistol that provides the tangible evidence for Brack's blackmail. Both of these women experience an intermediate relationship before their final relationship. That is, the unresolved relationship with Brack encourages Hedda's ultimate marriage to Tesman; and Thea's unsuccessful marriage to Elvsted encourages the more satisfying relationship with Eilert Løvborg. Each of these intermediate figures, whose presence threatens the new relationship, is a government official: the more distinguished Brack as judge, Elvsted as rural bailiff. *Hedda Gabler* suggests that within their disparate social and economic worlds, both Brack and Elvsted maintain economic power and authority, in contrast to the unfranchised Tesman and Løvborg.

In the brief section of dialogue in which Thea reveals to Hedda that the shadow of a woman from his past inhibits their relationship, Hedda learns her attraction for Eilert remains in force; and her consequent excitement, which for the spectator is not yet sufficiently motivated, manifests itself. At this point, the image of the red-haired singer functions for Thea, with Hedda's pretended agreement, as a hypothetical figure for the real woman of Eilert's past whom we later come to learn is Hedda herself. The triad—Hedda, Thea, Diana—represents both a social hierarchy (the haute bourgeoisie, the middle class, and the lower class) and a sexual hierarchy. Hedda is the most repressed; Thea stands ready to assume a sexual relationship with Løvborg outside of marriage; and Diana supports herself with her sexuality. In Eilert's imagination, Hedda is the most desirable within the bounds of this hierarchy, of course, and Thea and Diana function as substitutes when she is unavailable.

The missing—off stage—Diana provides an image of threat, a tangible competitor for Thea; and yet Hedda responds differently, at least until she learns the circumstances of Løvborg's death. In some sense, Hedda must identify with Diana as Eilert's sexual partner. Diana, outside of society, has the freedom Hedda can not imagine. That is, Diana is free from anxiety about the way in which society as a whole perceives her and she may, therefore, act out her sexual desires. She must, of course, be successful in displaying herself as a magnetic sexual object for the men who purchase her body, and, to be successful, she must build a reputation as an extraordinary erotic object. In some sense, she performs within her limited circle as the star attraction as Hedda must perform within her own set. In her initial dialogue with Hedda, Thea voices her misperception that Diana is the phantom figure—the *kvinne-skygge* (the shadow of a woman)—that stands in between Eilert Løvborg and herself. Thea's misconception, which Hedda reinforces, brings the two women from each end of both the social and sexual spectra together. Ironically, Thea's error in judgment points toward one of the most subtle and ironic alignments in this text. Both Hedda and Diana have been in relationships with Løvborg in the past, and the text suggests the probability that their relationships were coextensive. That is, the text puts forward the possibility that Diana was a sexual partner in the erotic adventures that Eilert confesses to Hedda. In that sense, Eilert maintains a verbal erotic relationship with Hedda and a physical relationship with Diana. At no point in the text does Hedda voice animosity or jealousy toward Diana, until Brack's report that Løvborg's death takes place in the prostitute's room. Hedda does, of course, respond with acute jealousy to Thea's involvement in Løvborg's work, the good comradeship of their relationship. And that jealousy is a primary motive in her destruction of the manuscript that they perceive as their child.

Ibsen's play represents an economy whose dynamics endanger its characters. It would be possible to talk about that economy as both sociopolitical and psychic. The text represents several dramatic characters' voiced perception of economic risk. However, the most important economic principles in this text present themselves subtly and indirectly in the various examples of economic exchange that operate in its action. Consider the various kinds of commodity that can serve as a vehicle of exchange or as collateral for borrowing in the late-nineteenth-century capitalistic world the text images: family property, the income from intellectual labor, the combination of intelligence, education, and the potential for academic achievement—that is, both Tesman's and Løvborg's future production and exchange of ideas in the university, actual labor in domestic service, and, finally, the sexual commodity of the body itself.

First of all, the drama establishes an idea of family property, family wealth. Eilert has inherited a substantial sum and has expended it. His behavior estranges him from his family and forbids his access to further family financial resources. We assume that Brack commands substantial private resources and economic influence. The scarcity of Tesman's family resources, the small annuity that Miss Tesman mortgages to furnish the Falk Villa, defines the limitations of his income. As well, the absence of General Gabler's capital and property (explained in the notes but undocumented in the final text) provides further representation of the need to exploit a vehicle of exchange other than capital or property. In terms of exchange, however, Løvborg has expended his capital for alcoholic and sexual pleasure. Diana, Hedda, and Thea—each within the circumstance of their own social strata—exchange their sexuality for the security provided by men. In that sense, their bodies constitute a kind of property that can be traded. Potential success—

public recognition and the promise of remuneration—constitutes a vehicle of exchange for Tesman or, at least, provides a kind of collateral that functions as the basis for the loan that purchases the Falk Villa. Tesman's situation becomes desperate because he has used an intangible resource in the purchase of Hedda. As well, the fragility of that resource becomes clear as the competition with Løvborg arises. Here the tangibility of Eilert's successful book, marked as well by the income that gives him the freedom to resume his dissolution, puts Jørgen at a potential disadvantage in this competition that is simultaneously, intellectual, economic, and sexual. The manuscript of Løvborg's second book, which Hedda destroys, is a tangible commodity; that is, it has an intrinsic value that Eilert could have exchanged in the future. Tesman marks that value in at least two ways. First of all, he claims that the manuscript is among the most remarkable he has ever read, and he also decries the illegality of Hedda's destruction of Eilert's manuscript as *property.* As the evidence or manifestation of promise, the book could function as collateral as well. The manuscript, for Hedda, of course, has value, not in a conventional economic sense, but as the physical evidence of Thea's relationship with Løvborg and this other woman's control over him. When she burns it, of course, she commits an act that, within the terms of the representation, has both symbolic and real consequences. The book is the commodity, the vehicle of exchange on which both Løvborg and Thea were to have built a future. For Eilert and Thea, of course, the manuscript holds both symbolic and economic value. It is the product of their relationship and holds value to them as a tangible proof of their mutual work; but its fundamental identity as a statement of his vision is a commodity that holds potential value in the commerce of their society. The manuscript, as potential book, is the instrument of the restitution of Eilert's position and the fulfillment of the promise his previous behavior invalidated.

Brack's potential exploitation of knowledge about Hedda's complicity in Løvborg's death clarifies another intangible vehicle of exchange: the use of knowledge and the threat of revelation to trade on sexual submission. Brack's threat, of course, exploits Hedda's fear of scandal, her fear of the exposure of behavior that would exile her from her social class. Hedda's destruction of her body answers that threat and removes her from that system of exchange.

These economic exchanges diffuse themselves in the psychic exchanges that transpire in the course of the play and its narrative context. Aunt Julle finds some kind of identity, some kind of functional grounding, in the care of others. Hedda experiences her life, most vitally, through her peculiar vicarious engagement with sexuality through Eilert. Mrs. Elvsted experiences her notion of reality through the language taught her by Eilert and, with Tesman, in the play's future, by reconstructing the destroyed book as a kind of memorial that will re-embody Løvborg himself. Tesman's leadership in that project defers his own work and redirects his efforts to restore Eilert's reputation. Each figure reconstitutes a sense of self-identity through his or her idea of another.

When we discuss dramatic realism and the theatrical form that Ibsen's writing helped to develop, we usually mark out the complexly interwoven references to the socioeconomic world that the dramatic figures appear to inhabit. A text appropriates, often unconsciously, ideological structures, linguistic schemes, and cultural biases. *Hedda Gabler,* as I've discussed, does indeed reveal the operation of a strict socioeconomic structure. That structure, however, reveals itself more in negation, in repression than in any other manifestation. When Hedda's energies attempt to voice themselves in behavior that lies outside of the circumference of her highly coded circle, she represses them. In her perception, the world has two perimeters: an inner perimeter that encloses her circle of friends to whose gaze her behavior must be acceptable, and an outer perimeter whose edges are accessible to almost all males but whose further limits have corrupted Eilert. Løvborg's stories open that world to her—ostensibly the world of Diana—but Hedda has neither the spatial nor the psychic freedom to move herself into these areas. The image of the circle itself is significant here. Hedda performs herself at the center of an arena and creates herself as an object for the perception of others. As well, that perception—the ceaseless observation of the rigidly coded potential witnesses—forms a trap as well as a field of play. The codes of the observers form a barrier that keeps her from moving through that boundary to the further perimeter. And, in that self-contained and self-containing world, Hedda uses the resources she finds. She destroys the commodity created by Løvborg with Thea, and she destroys the only commodity—her body—that she possesses once she discovers that this resource will no longer be hers to control. The irony of Hedda's situation derives from the fact that she does indeed desire access to the world forbidden her and yet she cannot survive in a world that she cannot dominate and control. Her own behavior, borrowed from the society in which she moves, forbids the intrusion of the world of reality except in the modes of circumlocution and symbolism. The very circumlocution Hedda requires embodies the restrictions that frustrate her.

The effort of the principal characters in *Hedda Gabler* to restructure their lives resolves destructively. Tesman seizes the opportunity of Hedda's extremity and her willingness to enter the marriage to place her as the central decorative emblem of his potential success. But that success remains hypothetical. As Tesman confesses in a rare moment of insight, "one should never go building castles in the air. . . . It was idiotically romantic to go and get married, and buy a house, just on expectations alone" (201).[8] Løvborg, with the concrete evidence of his restored intellect and moral reformation, builds a speculative future as a visionary historian in a deliberate effort to reconstruct his life. Thea, complicit in his fantasy, leaves the restrained security of her life, to follow him, both physically and imaginatively. The fragility of the material vehicle that embodies that fantasy—and the inadequacy of Eilert as its custodian—destroys their means of exchange in the commerce of this text. Hedda, alienated by the consequences of her own transaction, marriage into the middle class, attempts to restore her image of Løvborg as uncorrupted by the banality of bourgeois morality. Here she trades in what power she has—her ability to attract Løvborg sexually—and, in accepting the principles of that particular psychic economy both destroys him and puts herself in jeopardy as the victim of the sexual desire she provokes in Brack. *Hedda Gabler* conflates the capitalistic and psychic economies that consume its heroine.

7

Hedda Gabler (Tesman) and the Question of Character and Gender

I

When the discussion of Ibsen's dramaturgy shifted to the analysis of images, latent mythological content, or psychoanalytic substructure, the consideration of character in a conventional sense, from either an ethical or a conventionally behavioristic perspective, seemed inappropriate.[1] The mimetic bias of the late nineteenth century exemplified in the discussions of Ibsen by Bernard Shaw and the famous lectures on Shakespeare by A. C. Bradley provides the kind of literal reading of drama that much of twentieth-century criticism has rejected.[2] Shaw and Bradley valued those aspects of the dramatic text that allowed them to see a correspondence between the behavior of dramatic characters and their own understanding of human psychology, an understanding that was shaped by the social, scientific, and artistic attitudes of the late nineteenth century. While we need to see the limitations of that psychology and that aesthetic, we cannot erase the dynamic impact of the human actor/character as a principal part of the experience of the text in performance.

No critical system can erase completely the presence of the human image that occupies the space of the stage. When we posit analogies among the arts, we often discuss language as the medium of the playwright, language as equivalent to the painter's pigment. However, the painter/pigment : playwright/ language ratio is not accurate. The playwright's medium is the representation of figures in space who speak. The playwright, unlike the writer of prose fiction or epic poetry, cannot communicate directly to the reader or spectator, but writes words that are spoken by actors as the speech of individual figures. Each textual segment is mediated through the voice of a dramatized persona, who is usually physically present before the spectator. Each statement is communicated as the assertion, perception, image of a fictional persona. The representation of character—to use Dryden's metaphor, "the painting of the hero's mind"—is the representation of consciousness: the dramatization of a consciousness perceiving the scene, including other characters, and perceiving/imagining itself within that scene, and formulating, processing, or responding to that perception. The perception and mediation of images, grounded in the persona assumed by the actor (or an imagined actor), constitutes a primary aesthetic instrument at the playwright's disposal. While it is possible to use critical systems to construe latent organizational principles that operate independent of character, a major part of the data with which we work in that project comes to us through the agency of an actor representing a character. The statements that articulate the metaphoric or mythic referents that form the material of a substructure are themselves enclosed in an image of a speaker, a pseudohuman context that participates in the shaping of the individual image. Often, criticism—positivist, New Critical, structural, poststructural, or new historical—tends to treat these predications as free-floating statements disconnected from specific voices in concrete situations.

Rather than using *character* in A. C. Bradley's sense or within Shaw's terms, I am attempting to exercise a functional concept that is more equivalent to the formal schemas that the art historian E. H. Gombrich identifies in his discussion of representation in Western painting.[3] That is, I suggest that character—the figure in space and time—is not an object of representation but, rather a means of representation.

The plays of Samuel Beckett reveal the conventionality of the theatrical idea of *character* by revealing that character is less the mirroring of an entity whose counterpart or type exists in the objective world and is more a conventional formula that playwright, actor, spectator, and reader use to structure dialogue or speech. Beckett's texts bring to the foreground the assumption that character as subject is hypothetical, speculative, transitive. The notion of self or subject constitutes a fragile tissue that connects speaker to narrative, speaker to scene, and speaker to immediate moment. In Beckett's later drama, that connection—made by the actor and the spectator—is self-consciously hypothetical; and the spectator's acceptance of the character as the nexus of images of space and time should be tentative. After witnessing a performance of one of Beckett's plays, most spectators would agree that the text in performance leaves undisclosed far more information about its character or characters than it reveals. However, no dramatic character is ever a fully described or enacted "whole."

The dramatic text always represents character in metonymic fragments. For example, in a series of soliloquies in *Hamlet* we witness the protagonist at moments of philosophically speculative contemplation. We perceive these specific moments as unique, but representative, occasions, and we do not think that the character's conceptualization of these issues is limited to these few moments. We extrapolate an image of Hamlet as contemplative or philosophically speculative because we respond to these moments as representative segments of a virtual whole. While the *whole* is virtual, extratextual, a product of our imagination, the performed text stimulates us to produce that synthesized concept of character. While the amount of information that a performance of a Shakespearean play offers is far greater than that provided by any Beckett text, what Shakespeare does not disclose about Hamlet is greater than what he does. That is, the extrapolation made by the reader or spectator to create an image of character encompasses far more detail than the text holds.

If it were possible to graph the composition of the *whole* character established within a spectator's imagination, that chart would display the fragments of information provided by the text. The graph would also show, separately, additional data projected by the physi-calization of the actor, including the qualification of the textual data through speech and movement and the image of continuity supplied by the actor's representation of the character's intention. As well, the graph would illustrate the spectator's mediation of the presented infor-mation, an extrapolation of the data, which is based upon the organiza-tional principles or theoretical structures that he or she brings to the experience. In other words, the nature of that extrapolation depends upon the conceptual systems involved in perceiving the data. The frag-mented and equivocal nature of Beckett's images of character, space, and time exposes, more clearly than the work of any other playwright, the metonymic nature of dramatic images.

Ibsen's references to systems of determination—psychological, biological, socioeconomic—provide the spectator with images of char-acter that must also be synthesized in reception, but the amount of the data Ibsen provides is greater, and he suggests the theoretical con-structs by which that processing may be done. The spectators' share in processing the images of past, character, scene in Ibsen is proportion-ally greater than in Beckett, but the process they undertake is the same. At this moment in the course of aesthetic theory, we recognize that the construct, Hedda Gabler, is as artificial as the "character" behind the mouth in *Not I;* but the process of readerly assembly with which we build an image of Hedda Gabler in performance has more surface detail available to us than our analogous work with the figure of the woman in the Beckett play. In reading or watching the Beckett perfor-mance, we are more self-conscious about the degree to which we intervene in the project of reading figure (actor) and text as *character.*

One of the formal constraints demanded by Ibsen's own version of realism was the elimination of the character's direct, self-interpreting address to the audience. The consequence of this elimination increased what Auerbach has called the self-interpreting function of the text itself; that is, the suppression of direct communication to the audience (or reader) forces them to interpret the character's action and infer the motive from the language and gesture observed. The emergence of this kind of dramatic writing—the ostensible representation of behavior free of authorial intervention—soon became implicated in the development of a *realistic* acting style.

The texts of *Ghosts, The Wild Duck, The Master Builder,* and *Rosmersholm* invest images of the past profoundly in the present action. The material these texts provide their performers can become complicit with the evolving tendency of actors to supply a functional biography that fleshes out and even supercedes the limits of the language provided. In that sense, the actor's work, which produces a second text, underlays the spoken and supplies a consistent intentionality. *Hedda Gabler,* as I have noted earlier, yields much less information about the past. Muriel C. Bradbrook speaks clearly about the lacunae in this text:

> Hedda has neither self-awareness nor responsibility. Unlike Rebekka and Rosmer she has in their sense no inner life at all. . . . She is hardly self-conscious enough to suffer. Although she is once or twice seen alone, there is nothing in the play that could be called a soliloquy from her: she is shown entirely in action. It is a superb acting part: the greatest acting part that Ibsen created because the interpretation is left entirely to the actress, although material is generously provided. The action gives great opportunity and the maximum freedom, since the actress does not have to put across lines of self-analysis or explanation. All that is left to be conveyed in presentation. There is no frame, no comment. No judgement is passed upon Hedda, or even invited. The audience is not asked to respond with a verdict, and this objectivity of presentation, this neutral response is the most discomfiting thing about the play. . . . The whole play pivots upon Hedda but she herself is neither "placed" nor judged. She is a study in a vacuum.[4]

Professor Bradbrook here focuses upon what essentially is a textual phenomenon in Ibsen's play: the absence of language that displays the protagonist's introspection. Bradbrook argues that the textual interstices in *Hedda Gabler* license the actor's improvisation to fill in the missing data. That same absence of biographical exposition and introspective statement increases the text's and the character's vulnerability to interpretation and stimulates a wide range of disparate critical interpretation concerning the *character* of Hedda Gabler Tesman.

Criticism frequently, of course, focuses upon the ethical implications of Hedda's action. Within the last several decades, that interpretation extends from G. Wilson Knight's celebration of the dramatic figure and his reading of the "positive essence"[5] of her act to James Hurt's declaration that "to regard her act as 'courageous' in any real sense or her death as 'beautiful' would be to accept the same demented set of values Hedda has lived by."[6] Errol Durbach bases his reading of the play on a foundation that admits the interstices of the text. He states that "Hedda Gabler is enveloped in almost Pinteresque blankness. A phrase, a gesture, a sense of something left unspoken beneath broken sentences—we clutch at straws to make her whole or, bewildered by the force that drives her, attribute to her actions the motiveless malignity of Iago."[7]

Durbach's reference to Harold Pinter reminds us of the degree to which we have been trained, since *Waiting for Godot* and the early Pinter, to accept biographical or narrative gaps as part of a new logic of theatrical representation. This reference relates to my previous remarks concerning the obvious schematic nature of *character* in Beckett. The refusal of Ibsen's text to specify Hedda Gabler's motive with unambiguous clarity focuses our attention on the function of her manipulation rather than its motive. That is, we concentrate upon the expenditure of energy directed toward its object. We identify Hedda as the source of that energy and watch it operate. In the relationship between the two principals of Shakespeare's text that Durbach notes, Iago remains secondary to Othello. Our attention gathers special intensity as we see that protagonist assimilate or internalize the destructive power of Iago's subtle manipulation and enact his self-destructive course of action. Despite the intricate interrelationship between Iago and Othello, the primary subject remains Othello. In Ibsen's play, the relationship between Hedda and Løvborg is also intricate but radically less articulated; and, more significantly, the attention remains focused not on the object of manipulation but on the manipulator. We do not witness Løvborg's subjective appropriation or internalization of Hedda's scheme.

Ibsen's male protagonists discuss their ideas about vocation or develop physical projects that allow them to refer to themselves and their work in concise but often hubristic language. In those realistic plays that use a woman as the central figure—*A Doll's House, Hedda Gabler,* and *The Lady from the Sea*—Ibsen does not simply change the sex of the protagonist and develop analogous characters performing similar actions. These female protagonists conceptualize themselves in relation to the world they perceive very differently from Ibsen's male protagonists. Ibsen's male heroes develop personal stories that reveal their perception of the past and situate them at the center of comprehensive visions of reality, and, as well, they revise and transform these visions during the course of the performance. In *The Master Builder,* for example, Halvard Solness's relatively brief discussions of his career as a builder accumulate throughout the play to form a narrative of his career. In this history, he moves through four discrete time periods as the builder of churches, houses for the middle class, an idiosyncratic personal home that juxtaposes the form of a house with the tower of a church, and—finally, in the fourth stage—the castles in the air that are the product of his strange collaboration with Hilde. This collection of individual statements displays the master builder's struggle with the issues of responsibility, guilt, sexuality, self-identification, and time. Ibsen writes the speeches of Nora, Hedda, and Ellida Wangel with equally expressive language, but their dialogue does not suggest the kind of narrative consciousness typical of the playwright's male heroes. While Hedda Gabler commands keen verbal skills, she does not use narrative structures to build the kind of progressive, sequential statements of self-definition that her male counterparts implement as they build their images of vocation. In fact, the only reference Hedda makes to that kind of narrative scheme is her briefly held plan to make Jørgen into a politician. Self-formation in language is not Hedda's project. Nora does, of course, construct a type of narrative fantasy in her anticipation that Torvald will accomplish the wonderful action of assuming responsibility for the forgery. However, the narrative that Nora writes, in her imagination, builds upon Torvald, not her, as the principal agent of the story. In this fantasy, she perceives herself as spectator to this act and as the recipient of its altruism. At the final moment of the drama when Nora acts out the decision to leave, her vision of the future remains unarticulated because she perceives herself as yet unformed. The story of Nora's future, both in her mind and ours, remains unwritten, outside the field of vision of the play itself. Ellida's narrative of the past, the story of her former relationship with the American, operates as a partial history; and she is unable to use the material of her experience to forge a narrative that would give her a sense of reality in the present. Instead, she relies upon the compulsive act of swimming in the fjord. Ellida attempts to act out her relationship with the sea—itself an idiosyncratic personal image of the sexuality she cannot articulate in words—in the second-level substitution of swimming in the fjord, the point of mediation between the open sea and the stagnant pond. Ibsen's male protagonists seem to act in order to provide content for the narrative structures in which they identify themselves self-consciously. Ibsen's female protagonists identify themselves in symbolic gestures which they do not translate into narrative structures.

When Hedvig, the young girl in *The Wild Duck*, kills herself to recapture Hjalmar's love, she identifies herself in action; and we cannot, as spectators, extrapolate a narrative scheme that we imagine exists in her consciousness at the time of the suicide. Gregers suggests that she sacrifice the wild duck and, in that sacrificial act, clarify her love for the man she thinks of as her father. She substitutes herself for this wounded creature, not in a self-conscious representation of the story of the loss and regaining of her relationship with Hjalmar but as some kind of symbolic gesture that cannot be translated into a verbal structure. However, we see the ways in which Hjalmar immediately begins to write this event into his personal narrative; and Relling predicts his future use of this incident as the keystone to his self-conscious story-telling. In this juxtaposition of act and perception, we can identify a clear difference between Ibsen's representation of female and male processes of self-identification.

Hedda provides Ibsen's clearest example of a female figure who substitutes action, or verbal or physical gestures of performance, for the kind of narrative self-transformation that the male heroes exercise.

Hedda exercises self-formation only in her efforts to perform the role of General Gabler's daughter. She conceptualizes herself performatively rather than as the subject of a narrative. We rarely see Hedda in a situation in which she self-consciously explores her own consciousness. On the contrary, her self-consciousness, revealed in behavior, masks her emotions in a disciplined embodiment of the figure she wishes others to perceive as Hedda Gabler. In almost every moment of the play, we see the mask that Hedda assumes rather than the character underneath. Because the text does not represent the basic persona of Hedda Gabler, except in a very few instances, we extrapolate a sense of that figure on the basis of the ways in which we see the mask itself being manipulated. Ingmar Bergman's production of *Hedda Gabler* at the Royal Dramatic Theater at Stockholm in the late 1960s, which was reproduced in London with actress Maggie Smith, radically revised Ibsen's spatial scheme to theatricalize this phenomenon of behavior. This production developed a bisected stage that juxtaposed the difference between Hedda's private behavior and her performance of the animated, vivacious persona she displays in the public space of her drawing room.

Ibsen's stage directions and the implications of the language of the text provide some stimulus to our perception of the character's thought and emotion. However, Hedda's inner life remains out of sight or hearing. This inaccessibility functions rather like a performance of Hamlet that cuts the soliloquies and presents only those scenes in which Shakespeare's hero performs within his "antic disposition." The character of Hedda Gabler remains a product of our speculation. That is, as we process the surface details we perceive in the various postures she assumes, we hypothesize an idea of the figure underneath the mask. Unlike Ibsen's male protagonists, Hedda Gabler neither questions the nature of her own identity nor revises her interpretation of a personal history.

Consider two of those instances in which Hedda Gabler appears to speak sincerely rather than mask her self in a performance of highly controlled language. In the second act, as she discusses her previous relationship with Eilert, she confesses her cowardice to him.

When she does this, however, she describes her revelation of her real feelings in the past as the imitation of his confessions to her. She speaks honestly and, at the same time, examines her behavior, but she conceptualizes that action as the appropriation of the behavior of someone else. At the end of act 3, when she gives Eilert Løvborg one of her father's dueling pistols, she urges him to use it "beautifully." She envisions him performing an action, complete unto itself, that would answer her demand. If we can build upon her earlier terse statements, she sees that potential action as symbolic on two levels: first, the suicide would represent the power she holds over another person's destiny; and, second, it would embody Løvborg's freedom from the society she perceives as confinement. Significantly, Hedda does not perceive that action as the resolution or closure of a narrative but rather as a moment sufficient unto itself, "a heroic act." In her terms, this act would manifest beauty, free of the ludicrousness and farcicality of the bourgeois situation in which she finds herself trapped. Hedda's consciousness here appears atemporal; that is, she focuses upon the single moment almost as if it were the embodiment of a specific scene, a visual image, rather than a serial unit in a sequence of moments. In other words, she wishes to reconstruct the image of Eilert Løvborg as he existed in the earlier moment when his confessions to her defined a model of freedom from restraint that acted out her own *livskravet* (craving for experience). The most meaningful experience in Hedda's history has been the surreptitious conversations with Eilert Løvborg, through which she gained the illusion of access to a more tangible reality than she could experience. The repression imposed upon her by society and her own assimilation of those restraints denied her the ability to conceptualize an overt sexual relationship with Løvborg; and her energies were redirected into her interrogations of the young man whose activity included the sexual behavior forbidden her. Hedda Gabler's attempt to restore the reformed academic to his previous libertine identity constitutes an effort to return to the coordinates of that earlier moment. Hedda wishes the present to revert to the past; that is, she desires an atemporal conflation of two moments.

While Hedda's consciousness does not operate within a narrative process of conceptualization, she does prize language. Hedda's first dialogue with Brack emphasizes the barrenness of conversation with Tesman. Her longing for talk with the judge aligns with the significance she attaches to her secret meetings with Eilert. Her erotic energy has been displaced into the verbal encounter modeled by her interrogations of Løvborg, as I have emphasized. Eilert's return, and the possibility of being able to restore him to his previous identity, stimulates her behavior in act 2. The sordid reality, reported to her indirectly in act 3, spoils the more idealized Dionysian image their past conversations helped to build, and she revises her project into the image of his heroic suicide. Here the text suggests that part of the appeal of Løvborg's sexuality, for Hedda, has been its aggressive rejection of the strictures of bourgeois morality; and his suicide would be, in her imagination, the absolute transgression that would display his disdain for the ordinary and, as well, give him to her in an idealized memory that could never be transformed into the sordid.

Kindermord (child murder) constitutes a significant subaction in Ibsen's recurrent family drama.[8] In the typical Ibsenian drama, the male protagonist commits the child murder. In *Brand*, the priest hero elects to stay in the northern village to minister to his congregation instead of taking his sick child to a warmer climate where the boy would have a chance to survive. The sacrificed child remains a crucial component of Ibsen's essential drama, assuming a variety of different identities, both as an actual child and a metaphoric or illusory infant. In *The Wild Duck*, *The Master Builder*, and *Little Eyolf*, either the action or the expository narrative of the past includes the death of a child. In *Hedda Gabler*, the heroine burns Eilert's visionary manuscript, extending the metaphor in which Thea and Eilert define the prospective book as the child of their relationship. In *Rosmersholm*, the dead child is mediated into Rosmer's childlessness and, as well, into the nonexistent fetus with which Rebekka prods Beate into suicide so that Johannes will be free to marry her. In *When We Dead Awaken*, Rubek and Irene use the metaphor of child to conceptualize the sculpture that Rubek creates in replica of Irene. Rubek's transformation, and distortion, of that work of art functions as a surrogate sacrifice, an aesthetic and psychic *kindermord*.

In this version of Ibsen's core drama, Hedda appropriates Thea's and Eilert's conceptualization of the handwritten document as their child, and, within that specific language, she destroys the potential book: "HEDDA: [*throws one of the folded sheets into the fire and whispers to herself*]. Now I'm burning your child, Thea! With your curly hair! (*Throws a few more sheets into the stove.*) Your child and Eilert Løvborg's. (*Throws the rest.*) I'm burning . . . burning your child" (250). We need to think about this specific variation of the Ibsenian *kindermord*. Hedda maintains this act as a secret, shared only with Tesman, and by withholding this fact allows Eilert Løvborg to believe that he has lost the manuscript, at Frøken Diana's. This misconception leads him to create the lie for Thea about ripping it apart and throwing it into the fjord that he uses to convince her of the absoluteness of their separation. Eilert's ignorance of the real circumstances of the loss of the manuscript, of course, stimulates him to return to Diana's rooms to claim the package, an act that ends in his death. In this transformed version of an essential Ibsenian action, the female commits the metaphoric kindermord in fact; the male incorporates the action in his subjective reidentification of himself as a dissolute, flawed human being, unworthy of Thea's commitment.

Ironically, when she is burning the manuscript, fulfilling her intentions in behavior that is clearly symbolic, Hedda's language seems to represent her feeling most directly. At this climactic moment, Ibsen plays with an irony that may well be unself-conscious on the playwright's part. That is, Hedda does not have the means to form an independent image of herself as an agent in the world. Because she lacks that vocabulary, she cannot experience herself as a character within a personal narrative; that is, she cannot tell her individualized story as a figure in that world to which she is denied direct access. Ibsen's text not only disallows her ability to construct a narrative vision of her personal history, it positions her as the agent that destroys Løvborg's vision of the future. In place of that narrative scheme, the text allows Hedda to perceive herself and her relationship to Eilert in partial, visual images that are graphic but remain outside of a discursive system. Her identification of the manuscript as a child and her vision of Eilert Løvborg "with vine leaves in his hair" are striking visual transformations that are not implicated within a larger narrative structure.

As she thinks about Eilert, Hedda uses this arresting but undeveloped Dionysian image. We tend to think of this reference to Dionysian freedom as a synecdoche that she uses with a high degree of self-consciousness. That is, we respond to Hedda's allusion as a reference to a range of philosophical and historical ideas associated with the Dionysian, the bacchic, the nineteenth-century's appropriation of the Greek god as a model. I would argue, however, that Hedda's allusion is only literary or philosophic in a very unspecified, highly generalized sense. While it is tempting to believe that Ibsen invests this character with a highly sophisticated vision of Nietzsche's antithesis of the Dionysian and the Apollonian, the text itself gives us no evidence that she commands this kind of knowledge or that this paradigm infuses her language.[9] Hedda identifies and celebrates Løvborg's rebellion, not its ideology. Hedda's reference to the Dionysian is not discursive but, rather, visual as it isolates Eilert from the context of his personal history and perceives his behavior as an engagement in sensuous and sensual experience and willed rejection of conventional morality. When she hears the reports of Eilert's less heroic exploits, she abandons this imagery and focuses upon his suicide as a potentially aesthetic act. Whereas the male protagonists revise their narratives of the self, Hedda revises her visual image of the male whom she sees as the embodiment of freedom. She shifts from the romanticized image of Eilert as a Dionysian figure to locate him as the agent of an aesthetically performed suicide that would mark him as a hero.

When Hedda hears of Eilert's fatal injury, disguised in the circumlocution of Brack's initial report, she cries, "At last . . . a really courageous act!" (260). She sees her vision of the deed not as the culmination of a movement, but as an isolated manifestation of the will after a period of stasis. Why does she see that act as beautiful? This identification probably derives directly from the literary idealization of suicide in Goethe's *The Sorrows of Young Werther*. The attempted idealization of Werther's suicide, his return to the town, the use of the pistols that are "borrowed" from the married woman he loves—these analogies suggest that Ibsen uses details from Goethe's narrative to shape Hedda's sense of the potentially aesthetic nature of Eilert's act. While these analogies seem obvious, once they are pointed out, the fact that the play suppresses a specific reference to the novella is consistent with its practice of deleting or repressing material. If Hedda were to refer directly to Goethe's story, this allusion would give the spectator a sense of Hedda's perception of herself within a history, even a history of reading. The literary reference would violate the conventions of this characterization. While I make the connection between Hedda Gabler and *The Sorrows of Young Werther* to explain Hedda's idea of the potential beauty in an act of suicide, I don't mean to suggest that her obvious allusion to the novel characterizes Hedda as a well-read woman who uses Goethe's text to envision Løvborg's death. In fact, she and Brack ridicule the intensity and pleasure of Tesman's reading.

In these subtle uses of two earlier nineteenth-century works, the play characterizes Hedda as aware of their ideas in a popular sense, not in a profound or scholarly sense. Hedda's language suppresses the narrative content of these images from Nietzsche and Goethe and refuses to name either authors' works directly.

No other play in Ibsen's canon suppresses knowledge from its characters—and its audience—to the degree that this text withholds critical narrative facts. Ibsen's bold choice to place Hedda in the role of protagonist determines this suppression. As the central figure of this drama, Hedda's presence dominates the space represented, and the only words that can be spoken are those appropriate to an upper-middle-class drawing room in a city in western Europe at the end of the nineteenth century. Because the specific data of Ibsen's drama encompasses prostitution, sexual exploitation, adultery, drunkenness, theft, and deception—actions that can not be discussed openly—the basic narrative displays itself through indirection, implication, and linguistic disguise. That process—demanded by Hedda's presence and her social role—keeps much of the important material out of range of our perception. This censorship of language and the fact that Ibsen's text does not allow his female protagonist to conceptualize herself within a subjective narrative history ensures that the relationship between the ostensible reality outside the Falk Villa and the performance within remains a significant but obliquely represented connection.

Frequently feminist readings of Hedda have focused upon the fact that social circumstance so limits the range of her activity that she expends her intelligence and energy in destructive behavior out of sheer frustration. This interpretation of Ibsen's character has been appropriated by mainstream Ibsen commentary, and Martin Esslin writes, "Hedda Gabler ultimately constitutes a plea to allow women to develop their creativeness."[10] What this interpretation ignores is that the limited boundaries of Hedda's world are circumscribed by society, her own unwillingness to move outside of the concerns of her circle, and the fact that as a female in Ibsen's paradigmatic triad she can be embodied only as an object, not a subject. With the exception of her piano playing (the dance tune she plays immediately before shooting herself), the text of this play reveals no aesthetic or intellectual interests on the part of this heroine. Hedda maintains clear disinterest in the content of Eilert's work, spending no effort to read either the published book or the visionary manuscript. While her language suggests that she is jealous of Thea's relationship to Løvborg, her dialogue with the other woman does not reveal a desire to share in his work as Thea has done. Hedda's speeches display no sense that Eilert's writing projects his selfhood in any significant way. Hedda's aspirations encompass only a vision of herself as the center of an elite salon in this city and her efforts of self-formation remain limited to that role.

II

Ibsen wrote and rewrote the same essential story with a paradoxical combination of variety and consistency.[11] The hero's search for a comprehensive vision of reality that will position him as the principal subject of his environment constitutes the core of that recurrent narrative; and the two women signal the conflict between eroticism and responsibility. The basic action of *Hedda Gabler* does constitute a variation and expansion of the triangular pattern of the plays with a male protagonist. The relationship of this text to the well-established basic paradigm allows us to concentrate on the meaningful deviations from that model as Ibsen used it both before and after writing this particular play. In most variants of this triad, the male is central and the female figures operate to reveal his processes of self-identification; the female figures are essential, but secondary.

The two women in the Ibsen triad signal different stages of the erotic process as much as different attitudes toward sexuality. The seductive female represents the object of desire before the erotic encounter when yearning is acute, and the second female represents a substitute sexual object metamorphosed by the absence of desire by the time of the drama. The protagonist's impulse to build comprehensive visions of reality rivals sexual desire and, in each case, redirects that energy of sexual desire into the vocational project. At the point when the erotic female returns to the life of the hero, the vocational project has been the source of disillusionment rather than of satisfaction. In the temporal scheme of this drama, the return of the erotic female reembodies the power of desire, since the hero's renunciation of her and the continued presence of unsatisfied desire forms part of the narrative of the past. The return of this seductive female, for the most part, provides the occasion for the revelation and revision of that narrative. Much of the energy expended in the typical Ibsenian drama derives from the dynamics of the hero's desire and its repression. This core drama is, unequivocally, a male narrative in which the female characters become vivid primarily as projections of male desire and apprehension. Ibsen's masculine hero usually sacrifices his relationship with one of the females to implement his vocational project and accepts a life with the second female, who functions as an inadequate substitute and is usually sexually alienated from him by the time the action begins. The retrospective structure of Ibsenian realism allows the hero to rethink his choice; and the return of the erotic female offers him the illusion of a resolution to his present disillusionment, the illusion of a second chance at an erotic life.

If Ibsen had used this triad in *Hedda Gabler* according to his usual structural emphasis, Eilert Løvborg would function as the protagonist; Hedda would assume the role of the woman whose passion he renounced in his choice of vocation over the *livsglaed* (the "joy of life").[12] The diligent and faithful Thea would approximate the function of Aline, Beate, Rita, and Ella in defining the course of responsibility for this principal male figure. As well, Eilert Løvborg's death, described as a less ambiguous suicide than that reported in this play, would constitute a variation of a romanticized new vision of reality analogous to Brand's ascent into the Ice Church; Solness's triumphant climb to the top of the tower and the building of castles in the air with Hilde; Rosmer's suicide-marriage with Rebekka; Borkman's delusion of an expansive capitalistic empire; or Rubek's and Irene's apocalyptic ascent into the avalanche. In *Hedda Gabler*'s more ironic resolution, that idealized vision of the hero's death exists only in the temporary illusion of Hedda who, for a moment, sustains the illusion that Løvborg has killed himself in the act of heroism that she has requested. In a more typical variant, Løvborg's death would be joined more directly with Hedda's suicide in a complicit action shaped by the male. However, in *Hedda*, the mutual suicide of Rebekka and Rosmer, Rubek and Irene is fragmented into two separate actions: Hedda demands that Eilert kill himself "beautifully" and puts Løvborg at palpable risk with the gift of the general's pistol; and her death, fully formed in her imagination and enacted in a brilliant performance, substitutes for the inadequately realized incident in which Eilert is fatally wounded in a struggle with Frøken Diana. Ibsen's text emphasizes the second action by displaying it on the stage, although discreetly screened in the inner room, after giving the first action presence only in Brack's oblique narrative, a report that remains deliberately ambiguous. Here the male suicide, the final self-defining act, fails; and the female reenacts it in a successful resolving gesture of self-formation and defiance.

Like Johannes Rosmer, Halvard Solness, John Gabriel Borkman, and Arnold Rubek, Eilert Løvborg ends his life disillusioned about his vocational project. Rosmer, Solness, and Rubek resolve their lives in a suicide or, at least, put themselves deliberately at risk; and, each enacts this movement in accord with the woman who has returned to his life.

In *Hedda Gabler,* the man returns to the experience of two women he renounced earlier. Within the time scheme of the play, Eilert is, technically, in the city when Hedda returns from her wedding journey. However, in terms of the use of scenic space, Eilert returns to Hedda's experience by entering the place she dominates. When Eilert maintained his curious relationship with Hedda earlier, he based that liaison on his secret confessions of sexual misadventures—stories that ostensibly included his relationship to Frøken Diana. The text suggests, but does not confirm, that Hedda's knowledge of Frøken Diana comes directly from Eilert's confessions to her. As I discuss in chapter 5, Ibsen's text aligns Hedda and Diana as joint figures who share his sexuality: Diana physically, and Hedda verbally. When he returns to the city after his restorative stay in the provinces, Eilert resumes a relationship with both women that reenacts, with critical differences, that same complicit triad.

If *Hedda Gabler* were typical of Ibsen's dramas, we would have some knowledge of the content of Eilert Løvborg's writing or, at least, some sense of the way his historical discourse uses ideology to generate a vision of reality. We would, as well, have sufficient information to hypothesize a relationship between Løvborg's notion of himself in relationship to his historical vision. In this case, the sexual narrative of Eilert's confessions to Hedda, the recently published book, and the new manuscript would document the stages of this hero's perception and revision of reality, analogous to the stages of building that Solness articulates to conceptualize his relationship to divine and social responsibility. However, *Hedda Gabler* places the character that would normally stand at the center in the typical Ibsen play in an important, but not central, location. Whereas the ideological content of Løvborg's writing functions as the clearest, most intelligent, politically radical, and potentially influential vision of the world in this play, Ibsen's text reveals almost nothing of its ideas. Ibsen's notes for *Hedda Gabler* make the connection between Hedda's earlier conversation and Eilert's new book very clear. One of these textual segments has Tesman state that, "The new idea in E. L.'s book is that of progress resulting from the comradeship between man and woman." In the course of writing the play, the playwright eliminated this telling reference that relates the historian's vision of the future to a new comradeship between men and women. In this earlier, unused reference, Ibsen clearly invests the past relationship between Løvborg and Hedda with ideological value by making these two good comrades the prototype for his model of a new society. But the playwright did not clarify that connection in the actual text of the play itself, and, consequently, readers and spectators do not see the radical sexual politics in Eilert Løvborg's vision of the future. This ellipsis accomplishes at least two things: first, it removes Hedda as a partner in Eilert's work in eliminating their earlier relationship as a prototype for the future; second, this omission removes the only specific characterization of the significant manuscript so that the content of this document remains unknown, inaccessible to us. Through this omission and Hedda's own disinterest in Eilert's writing, the text removes the possibility that Eilert's vision of reality articulates an idealized vision of a new future that would reenact his relationship with her.

In *Rosmersholm*, which precedes this drama, Ibsen posed the possibility of a progressive, liberal, altruistic union between a man and a woman. The vocational project in that play projects itself as a mutual effort in which Johannes Rosmer and Rebekka West would embark on an idealized, educational mission. However, sexual desire—repressed in the past and articulated in the present—destroys the possibility of that liberal objective. In *Hedda Gabler*, Ibsen removes Hedda from any connection to Løvborg's project other than as its destroyer. This drama, therefore, becomes even more bitter and ironic than *Rosmersholm* because while the liberal vocational project shared by male and female proves equally impossible, the earlier text, at least, establishes that objective as an ideal. In the more drastic revision of that essential dynamic in *Hedda Gabler,* the text removes the principal female from the vocational, visionary project and moves the document that articulates that ideology out of view. Consequently, while

Rosmersholm opens up the possibility of its principal female's succeeding as a social reformer, an active force in society, *Hedda Gabler* circumscribes the range of its heroine's action more tightly. In the earlier play, Rebekka is educated by her progressive mentor, Dr. West, but she is eventually immobilized as she comes to learn that he was actually her father and that their sexual relationship was incestuous. In *Hedda Gabler,* the figure of the dead General remains in the focus of our attention because his portrait dominates the space, but his relationship with his daughter remains unclarified. Part, at least, of Rebekka's freedom derives from her status outside of society; and Hedda, of course, is circumscribed within the requisite decorum of appearances demanded by her more aristocratic inherited status. Both Hedda and Rebekka, however, are destroyed by the sexual dynamics of Ibsen's essential drama.

Clearly, Eilert Løvborg's vision of the future is not the subject of this play. Ibsen's choice to reposition the presentation of this narrative in order to emphasize one of the females in *Hedda Gabler* was, I believe, a bold and audacious act. The product of this reconfiguration is a fascinating, if highly problematic, dramatic text: "problematic" because the structural revision of the triad puts a character in the center of the theatrical space who is unable to speak the language of the Ibsen hero. In other words, Ibsen places this figure center stage—in the place of the highly self-conscious male hero—but his text prohibits her from assuming that revelatory self-consciousness. Even in this new position, the female figure remains elusive, inaccessible, puzzling. Like Hilde, Rebekka, and Irene, Hedda Gabler is brilliant, fascinating, and seductive; like these other dramatic figures, Hedda is an object of male desire. The typical Ibsen protagonist displays male desire, the suppression of that desire, and its displacement into the creative project. As I have discussed, this core drama includes a self-destructive resolution in which the principal male invites the erotic woman to participate in a final suicidal act, which substitutes for the vocational project, but which is transformed in language into a sexual liaison or marriage. However, the "marriages" of *Rosmersholm* and *When We Dead Awaken* and the sexual fantasy of Solness's castles in the air are, in deed if not in language, reenactments of the earlier sexual renunciation of these women.

The highly self-conscious language of Ibsen's male protagonists give us sufficient evidence to build a vision of their inner life. Solness, Rosmer, Allmers, and Rubek articulate their desire assertively, and in dialogue they reveal their disillusionment. They voice dissatisfaction with the asexuality of their marriages and see that barrenness as a consequence of their rejection of the *joy of life* for vocation; and they also respond to the erotic woman in positive assertions of renewed desire even if it is expressed in oblique language. Desire forms the center of these plays. Brand, Julian, Solness, Rosmer, Allmers, and Rubek manifest an acute desire for a comprehensive knowledge, a powerful understanding of reality. That intellectual, self-defining desire competes with a strong erotic sexual desire that is almost equally powerful. I use the phrase "almost equally powerful" because in Ibsen's dramaturgy, repression inevitably succeeds. In these male-centered dramas, the hero renounces the erotic female twice. The narrative of the past includes the hero's initial sexual denial of the female object of desire, and the present action includes his self-destructive reformation of desire into a death that he describes as marriage. While that translation of terms appears to work for the protagonist, the reader's or spectator's response often includes an ironic perception that interprets the hero's final choice as one more illusion, one more evasion of the demand of sexual desire.

The fact that Ibsen's text positions the character of Hedda in the role of the protagonist and then refuses to allow her the self-formative function of creating a narrative almost serves as an ironic documentation of the theories of Luce Irigaray, the French psychoanalyst who extends and critiques Lacan's neo-Freudian theory. The important aspect of that theory for this argument is the idea that discourse itself, which replicates the primacy of the male psyche, excludes the very possibility of the female as a speaking subject. Irigaray quotes Jacques Lacan: "There is no woman who is not excluded by the nature of things, which is the nature of words." The feminist argument that Irigaray advances identifies discourse, narrative, "logically" sequential assertions as replications or representations of the male psyche. When women speak within these structures, they borrow or temporarily inhabit a subjectivity that denies their reality as subjects. Ibsen's refusal to allow Hedda the kind of narrative consciousness he invests in his male protagonists aligns with his representation of her as the object of desire rather than the desiring subject. Ibsen's text disallows its female protagonist the possibility of self-formation in language.

The renunciation, repression, and displacement of desire in these texts is a male action. Agnes, Hilde, Rebekka, and Irene represent sexually willing females, highly erotic and eroticized objects of desire.[13] Consider, for example, the language in which Ibsen's text describes Solness's encounter with Hilde in the anteroom of her father's home—the imagery of bending her head back and kissing her many, many times. As well, think of the image of Irene posing nude before Rubek as he directs his sexual energy into modeling the wet clay. The text of *Hedda Gabler* consistently emphasizes Hedda's physical beauty, and the attention of both Tesman and Frøken Julle directs us to her body, newly voluptuous, hidden by her clothes but—in Tesman's words—visible to him who has "the occasion." However, in the revision of the essential Ibsenian drama, Ibsen shifts the act of sexual renunciation from male to female; and the critical sexual sacrifice of the past becomes Hedda's unwillingness to have a physical sexual encounter with Eilert Løvborg and ends their relationship by threatening to shoot him.

The absence of a desire for self-identification in a creative project that would embody a vision of reality and the absence of a strong sexual desire that opposes this vocational project makes the dramatic figure of Hedda Gabler both atypical and, in my earlier terms, problematic as protagonist. Ibsen develops an image of the hero's inner life through the direct and indirect assertion of these antithetical desires. Ibsen's psychology, whatever its source, bases itself on this oppositional paradigm. His male heroes see themselves as perceiving subjects, responding to, mediating, and representing the external world. They define themselves as comprehending and desiring subjects. The language that Ibsen's text provides for Hedda suggests that this figure perceives herself primarily as an object, a highly valued social and erotic icon who forms the center of a hypothetical circle of admiring attendants. In the experience the play gives her, Hedda Gabler seems most herself, most content within the appreciative sight of Judge Brack. As the object of value, whom people solicit, Hedda senses a kind of power, the authority that admiration and desire invest in her. However, she recognizes that her power as the principal object of desire in her world is, indeed, temporary, and she realizes that her play of authority as an iconographic figure has a limited life.

Because Hedda refracts desire, rather than embodying desire, she deflects the energy directed toward her; and the psychic energy of the play remains unsettled throughout the performance. None of that energy comes to rest but, rather, returns to its source unsatisfied. In almost all of Ibsen's plays, the protagonist acts out an unsatisfactory sexual life. However, in the plays with male protagonists, we witness the articulation of desire, the evidence of sexual repression, and the attempt, through language and gesture—as in Solness's ascent of the tower—to create an image that unifies the desire for sexual experience and the desire for knowledge. Even if that attempt is futile, the text and its performance expend energy in their representation of the pursuit of impossible objectives.

In *Hedda Gabler,* the protagonist has neither opportunity nor desire to unify sexual pleasure and the pleasure of knowledge. One of the consequences of shifting the center of focus in *Hedda Gabler* to one of the two women is the displacement of this desire from the center to the periphery. Hedda's presence constitutes a magneticism that attracts, but her intense concentration on her own situation does not encompass a keen desire for others. Her wish to manipulate Eilert, to exert power over him, is not the equivalent of Solness's desire for Hilde. The exception, of course, is the covert dialogue with Eilert Løvborg in act 2, in which she both moves toward Løvborg and reenacts desire and the repression of desire simultaneously. Throughout the play, however, the energy that Hedda expends articulates her dissatisfaction and distances her from those who desire. Consequently, in this text the protagonist's principal action is one of alienation, estrangement, retreat, escape from the strictures of relationship rather than movement toward a sexual object.

Looking at this triadic drama from another perspective, it is possible to see Hilde's function in *The Master Builder* as analogous to one aspect of Hedda's relationship to Eilert Løvborg. In her description of the event at Lysanger ten years earlier, Hilde articulates a vision of Halvard Solness that is clearly different than his own self-perception. Her idealization of his triumph articulates what he wishes the moment had been; and in her memory she also positions his encounter with her as a socially transgressive but exciting act, the mature man kissing the preadolescent female. She also claims that at this point he promised that he would return for her and carry her off to a magic kingdom; that is, that she would be able to escape from her ordinary life through his efforts. Hedda, as well, articulates—although less distinctly—her vision of Eilert Løvborg at an earlier point in the relationship. That vision, like Hilde's image of a "robust conscience," released from guilt, perceives Eilert as free of the constraining strictures of society. At this later, renewed stage of their relationship, Hedda, like Hilde, wishes to stimulate this man to recapture his earlier, triumphant, freer selfhood. Both Hilde and Hedda voice perceptions of the man who functions as a hero for them that are antithetical to the more limited, fearful, "realistic" perceptions of another woman, Aline or Thea. Their articulation of this vision contributes to the man's decision to put himself at risk. Both Solness and Løvborg destroy themselves because of the impetus to act that is defined for them by a highly energized woman. As I have noted, Ibsen organizes *The Master Builder* so that the final assertion of the male is more self-formative and, as well, more integrally complicit with the female.

The differences between *The Master Builder* and *Hedda Gabler*, of course, embody the significant issue in this discussion. In *Hedda Gabler*, the final action of the male—which, in this case, is the ambiguous, confused, and failed implementation of the course the woman outlines for him—is something that she experiences. That is, our focus is not upon the male act but upon the female's response to it and, more significantly, to her reenactment of the project he failed to complete satisfactorily, or, within the language of this text, *beautifully.*

Both plays achieve a unified structure by juxtaposing two events: the narrated or recollected event and its reenactment. In *The Master Builder,* that memory and reenactment is structured precisely with the rite in which the master builder places a wreath on the top of the tower he has built. In *Hedda Gabler,* the moments of the past and the present are more diffused. Hedda experiences the world through the displacement of her identification with Løvborg's "free" behavior, his dissoluteness; she attempts to recreate that experience by witnessing him become that figure once again, as a manifestation of her power over him. *The Master Builder* ends ambiguously, but the sense of ultimate accomplishment, of self-assertion is clearly present along with the irony. Løvborg's death is ludicrous, represented in the text as almost pure irony. Hedda's appropriation of the idealized act attempts to reconfigure it and does, clearly, hold some sense of assertion, self-formation, but it is also contextualized by irony.

Hilde's function in *The Master Builder* is to articulate a critical aspect of the hero's program, his self-formative narrative, the ego-centered but dynamic project that is inhibited by guilt, fear of aging, and a latent, unarticulated sense of regret over denied sexuality. The rotation of the triad in *Hedda Gabler,* as I've remarked, shifts our awareness of Løvborg's self-formative project out of our focal range; and the revision of the text censors the barest suggestions of its content. Consequently, the focus remains on the articulation of the impulse to act, on the erotic object who uses that eroticism to define the male's course of action—action whose significance is left unspoken apart from its meaning as an image for her. Because the act Hedda provokes is of use only to her, only to fulfill her liberating image, it is empty of actual content. The act she articulates is, in many senses of the concept, a negation. That is, her demand for Eilert Løvborg's suicide is a negation of her own subjectivity in that she asks him to act for her, to create an action that she can enjoy vicariously. Hedda subordinates her own identity to her vision of his "heroism." She wants Løvborg to make a gesture that constitutes itself as an aesthetic product, a deed that exists not for the agent but for the witness, an act that nullifies the self as subject and establishes the self as object. Hedda asks Eilert to commit an act that terminates his life—his biography, his narrative—as the final segment of that story. Her sense of this resolving act subsumes the narrative itself in a final, visual image.

Erotic females in Ibsen—Furia, Hjørdis, Helena, Hilde, Rebekka, Asta, Irene—wield power over the male protagonists. These men perceive them ambivalently, reacting to their erotic stimulus and repressing that desire because otherwise it would be all-consuming. Ibsen's heroes almost inevitably renounce the female who combines eroticism and virginity, and they sustain desire for them at a distance, where their eroticism functions only as image, memory, illusion. Solness suppresses even the memory of the virginal Hilde. When the female erotic object takes the central place in *Hedda Gabler,* that renunciation, that suppression, becomes a function of the text as a whole, not merely that section of the text that provides the action for the principal male. Hedda becomes, therefore, a person who exists for others and for herself as a glorious object; but she is not a desiring subject. Her motive is to be an object of desire for others, an object of *unachieved* desire. In a sense, Ibsen's text does not formulate Hedda as a full subject. Ibsen, as much as the bourgeois society that he attacks, circumscribes the action allowed this character. To speak more accurately, the triadic paradigm to which Ibsen's writing was subject denies Hedda the power of comprehensive self-consciousness. Of course, in play after play the Ibsen text suggests that the comprehensive visions the male protagonists generate are ultimately illusory and instable. In *Hedda Gabler,* the ironic picture of Thea and Jørgen attempting to restore Løvborg's manuscript in a project that exceeds their vision reveals that the male narrative consciousness has no more lasting presence than does the female gesture. Ibsen's male protagonists, however, have the opportunity to inhabit, for a moment, the illusion that their narrative has presence and value.

Applying the theories of Luce Irigaray once again, it would be possible to claim that *Hedda Gabler* presents a woman who has been unable to perceive herself as a subject because her processes of conceptualization, from the moment she learns language, have been framed in a language in which subjects are male; she has been forced by culture to appropriate, for temporary stability, a series of predications that she knows, when she uses them, are false. I would reframe this proposition. Ibsen denies his female protagonist the desire to build narratives of the self in which the subject is central, in which the perceiving subject attempts to position himself at the center of a vista in which he can comprehend, within sight, "all the glories of the world." In the draft of this play, Ibsen sites the Falk Villa more specifically on an elevation that commands a view of the fjord and its islands from the terrace immediately outside the glass door to which Hedda seems drawn periodically during the action. Anyone familiar with the Ibsen canon would recognize the ways in which his male characters use the physical reality of such a vista to conceptualize their comprehensive grasp of the objective world. The careful deletion of the simple reference in which Hedda remarks to Brack that she has walked on the terrace and seen its view over the fjord documents the more inclusive editing of Hedda's relationship to the world at large that Ibsen's control over this text manifests.

The text of Ibsen's *Hedda Gabler* displays the figure of its female protagonist in a project of self-formation that is radically atemporal and nonverbal. One of the conventions of dramatic literature is the creation of an image of character as a dramatic figure's self-formative predications accumulate during the course of the play or performance. Those self-defining or self-referential statements occur, of course, within the context of the perception of the figure by other subject-characters. Hedda's language demonstrates an awareness of her existence as an object perceived by others. Society, according to Hedda, perceives its objects, defines its membership, according to codified restrictions that are largely negative. In her vicarious identification with Eilert Løvborg and her failed attempt to manage his heroic suicide, Hedda attempts to maneuver him into an act that would express her own hostility toward social constraint. This text clearly and deliberately emphasizes the codification of behavior, neatly articulated in the repeated predication, "people don't *do* that sort of thing." Doing, acting, behaving outside of the proscribed range devalues the transgressor. In the case of woman, that break in the rules destroys her worth—as a legitimate object of desire and as a viable commodity in the sexual economy.

Consider the context in which Hedda performs her final gesture. Thea and Tesman are working on the reconstruction of Eilert's manuscript. Hedda, who has come to the point of recognizing the futility of depending upon her idealized vision of Løvborg as hero, ironically perceives Thea's compound dependency as this woman acts out an attenuated replica of her relationship with Løvborg in the project of restoring her romanticized image of the dead man with Tesman. Brack, who threatens Hedda's loss of authority over her own body, waits patiently down stage. Hedda kills herself in a representation of the death she planned for Løvborg in a shocking, unexpected, radically transgressive act that is beyond the comprehension of those who witness it. From one perspective, we could identify this act as Hedda "speaking (as) woman" in Irigaray's terms: an attempt "to disrupt or alter the syntax of discursive logic, based on the requirements of univocity and masculine sameness, in order to express the plurality and mutuality of feminine difference and mime the relations of 'self-affection.' "[14] On the other hand, we could also perceive Hedda's suicide within a different context as an event called for in the dynamics of Ibsen's paradigmatic triad, as the clear and irrevocable renunciation of the *erotic female*. When the male protagonist is no longer alive to complete that task or seduce her into a complicit suicide, as Rosmer persuades Rebekka or Rubek convinces Irene, the text or the playwright must perform that act. It is plausible to speculate that Ibsen's sympathy for those oppressed by the hypocrisy of middle-class morality and the jeopardy of late-nineteenth-century capitalism would invest Hedda's suicide with a sense of self-assertion that would celebrate its freedom to transgress the staid formalism of that drawing room and all it embodies. However, Ibsen's skepticism about the ultimate value of any self-assertion would underlay that celebratory sense with irony. As well, the obsessive hold of the sexual paradigm on the playwright's text would provide some comfort in the fact that one more sexual threat had been silenced.

8

Narration, Storytelling, Speakers, and Listeners

The text of *Hedda Gabler* uses an idiosyncratic model of communication in several instances that in a single use would not be notable but in the presence of several variants demands attention. This paradigmatic situation includes one person speaking a narrative while another listens. In itself, this rhetorical situation constitutes a conventional dramatic situation particularly useful to processes of exposition. Curiously, in the model I identify in *Hedda Gabler,* Ibsen adds a third person who is present but does not listen to the exchange between the two others. Moreover, Ibsen's triangular model of a speaker, a listener, and a present third person who does not hear constitutes, principally, a memory of a rhetorical situation. For example, as she reveals more to Hedda than she wishes, Thea speaks of a series of conversations between herself and Løvborg in the presence of Bailiff Elvsted that eventually developed into Thea's assistance with Løvborg's writing. Of course, Thea's revelation to Hedda takes place in a situation in which she and Hedda speak with the presence of Tesman nearby in the inner room.

Like Thea's memory of her friendship with Løvborg, Hedda's memory includes Løvborg as speaker and herself as listener. In this memory, Løvborg tells stories of sexual adventures; with Thea, he speaks "of an infinite number of things" in a process that makes her aware of herself as a human being. The conversation with Hedda is erotic; the conversation with Thea is ideological or conceptual. However, both situations contain a speaker, Løvborg, who uses language to excite his listener. And this narrator presents the listener with details of a world to which she has no other access. That is, the female listener uses these narratives to appropriate a reality, within her imagination at least, that would otherwise be forbidden her or held inaccessible. In the draft version of this conversation, Hedda uses the expression: "To me you were like a messenger from a forbidden country."[1]

The presence of the third person constitutes a puzzling but significant component of both of these variants of the paradigmatic model: General Gabler or Bailiff Elvsted, whose attention is directed to some individual concern, but whose presence also authorizes or legitimizes the relationship of speaker and listener within the limits of social convention that would make their wholly private discourse impossible. Ibsen's text reminds us of that restraint. Recall that when Hedda declares that Eilert may prefer to remain with her when Tesman goes off with Brack to the party, Tesman objects to the idea that she could, unattended, entertain Løvborg, and Hedda explains that Thea will be present and eases her husband's obvious discomfort.

This model of speaker and listener also characterizes the male as a figure whose behavior takes him outside of convention; the female displays moral restraint even though that restraint enacts radically different motives. Hedda's restraint takes the form of the circumlocutions in which she asks Løvborg explicit questions with implicit language. Her ultimate restraint takes the form of renouncing him, threatening his life, when he attempts to move their relationship into physical sexuality, and, of course, terminating their surreptitious meetings in the presence of General Gabler. Thea's restraint operates through her unvoiced desire for Løvborg to reform: "He left off his old ways. Not because I asked him to. I never dared do that. But he knew all right that I didn't like that sort of thing. And then he gave it up" (194). Hedda's sexual renunciation of Løvborg, according to her statement to him, may be the manifestation of her cowardice. In any case, both Hedda and Thea function as instruments of accepted moral codes even if they implement that restriction differently. Of course, when Hedda and Løvborg do speak privately, outside of the presence of the third party, the consequences are disastrous to both. In a sense, when the relationship of Thea and Eilert leaves the implicit control of Elvsted's presence, they put themselves at risk as well.

Hedda Gabler contrasts that basic triangular model of masked conversation with the image Hedda develops in her conversation with Judge Brack at the beginning of act 2: Here she describes being caught within the relentlessly claustrophobic situation of hearing Jørgen Tesman speak of the history of Western culture in general and the domestic crafts of the Middle Ages from morning until night. Brack, of course, introduces the idea of a third party's joining that couple; and the two of them play with that image of the addition of an "amusing conversationalist . . . [who is] . . . not in the slightest degree a specialist." When the play actually dramatizes conversations among Hedda, Brack, and Tesman, we witness a hidden dialogue between Hedda and Brack. The relationship of Hedda and Brack is defined, subtly but explicitly, as based upon the kind of conversation that is sustained by those in their circle; and Tesman's inability to use this vocabulary demonstrates his difference from that group. Consequently, the image of the triangular relationship, besides its more explicitly erotic component, also uses the model of a covert dialogue in the presence of a third party. Here Hedda and Brack become the couple whose conversations remain unheard—or at least not understood—by Tesman.

We need to think more profoundly about the significance of this model. In the first place, the triangle that contains a dialogue among two of its participants presents the image of a controlled erotic encounter that limits its sexuality to language. The presense of the third party—be that third party General Gabler, Bailiff Elvsted, or Jørgen Tesman—ensures that the relationship will not break through the limiting bonds of language to become physical gestures. Hedda contrasts the possibility, for her, of maintaining that kind of triangular situation in which the dialogue is covert with the impossibility of physically leaving the marriage with Tesman for another kind of liaison. The restraint of sexuality—ultimately, within the terms of this text, the impossibility of overt sexuality—invests the basic model with an erotic charge that is intensified in its repression. The antithetical model—the dialogue between Hedda and Tesman, in which there is no prohibition or protection against overt sexual behavior—lacks that reciprocal exchange of displaced erotic energy. When Hedda explains her motives in burning Løvborg's manuscript, she allows Tesman to interpret her behavior as the manifestation of a sexual awakening provoked by her love for him. She uses this idea, however, as a subterfuge, as a performance that masks the absence of any sexuality in her use of the marriage. She uses the appearance of her passion for Tesman as a circumlocution that hides her actual motive in burning the manuscript, a motive that encompasses her acute sexual jealousy of Thea's relationship with Løvborg. Her pretended feelings for Tesman provoke him to protect her by being silent about her crime.

The most significant representation of this model of communication comes at that moment in act 2 when Hedda and Løvborg use the photograph album, filled with pictures of the Tesman honeymoon, to mask their conversation from Brack and Jørgen, who talk, drink, and smoke in the inner room. Hedda and Løvborg self-consciously mark the fact that this situation replicates the series of afternoons in which they would sit on the corner sofa, speaking intimately, while General Gabler sat, with his back to them, reading a newspaper at a window across the room. In this important dialogue, therefore, we see both the mask, Hedda's pretense of showing Løvborg the photos performed for Tesman and Brack, and a rare honesty of language as Hedda relives the earlier experience. In Hedda's imagination, the experience she realized in these concealed conversations seems to remain the most vital segment of her life. At least, we see her engaged with the memory of a moment from the past with a greater display of energy than at any other point in the text.

Løvborg describes the ways in which he would confess his adventures with her:

HEDDA: ... My memory is that we were two good companions [comrades is a better translation]. Really sincere friends. (*Smiles.*) You were especially candid.

LØVBORG: You were the one who wanted it like that.

HEDDA: When I think back to that time, wasn't there something attractive, . . . something courageous too, it seems to me . . . about this . . . this secret intimacy, this companionship that no one even dreamed of.

LØVBORG: There was, Hedda. . . . When I came up to your father's in the afternoons. And the General used to sit by the window, reading the papers . . . his back towards us. . . .

HEDDA: And we sat in the corner sofa. . . .

LØVBORG: Always with the same magazine in front of us. . . .

HEDDA: Yes . . . for want of an album.

LØVBORG: Yes, Hedda . . . and then when I used to confess to you . . . ! Told you things about myself that none of the others knew at that time. Sat there and admitted that I'd been out on the razzle for whole days and nights. For days on end. Oh, Hedda . . . what power was it in you that forced me to reveal all those things? (222)

Here Løvborg uses the word *skriftet*, the same word used for religious confession. The basic noun *skrift* can refer to writing, publication, literature (narration), written or oral testimony; and with the adjective *helige* the word becomes Scripture, as in the Holy Scriptures or the Holy Writ. I introduce that range of meaning here in order to weigh the particular value that the phenomenon of language forming narrative holds in this drama, especially in this particularly revelatory scene. Earlier I defined the nonnarrative aspect of Hedda's self-conceptualization as radically different from the male heroes who use elaborate schemes or verbal or aesthetic representations of reality to position themselves in a comprehensive image of the world. The prototypical crisis in Ibsen's plays, of course, is precisely the failure of that attempt to appropriate reality within what I've called a personal myth. The words of this particular dialogue represent a younger Hedda, who describes herself as forbidden to experience Løvborg's world, using his stories to gain some view, not a comprehensive vision, but, at least, a "glimpse" of a world—or a particular set of experiences—which society, manifesting itself through her fear of social censure, would keep hidden from her.

Løvborg emphasizes that these narratives of sexual revelation were driven by Hedda's oblique questioning, "subtly disguised" in the circumlocution required by the fact that she cannot frame questions by using certain words that would more directly point to the specifics of what he does or experiences during those days and nights of licentious behavior. In Løvborg's mind, the coercion operating in those questions constitutes a power in Hedda to which he, and his language, are subject. The words are his, but the impulse to speak comes through Hedda's presence and her desire to hear his narrative, a narrative that we can assume is predominately sexual in its content. The secrecy of their relationship—which is acted out in the presence but not the hearing of General Gabler—protects their verbal intimacy from the knowledge of others. As well, the presence of this third party imposes a control that keeps the relationship from shifting from the verbal eroticism of their conversation to physical sexual behavior.

This scene between the former friends reveals Hedda's refusal to make the transition from the eroticism of language to a physical sexual relationship and clarifies that her response to Løvborg's spoken desire for her was her threat to shoot him. This incident marked the dissolution of their earlier relationship. Ibsen develops Hedda's self-assessment of her cowardice in an economical use of three declarations in this later scene. First of all, she declares it was her cowardice (her fear of scandal) that kept her from fulfilling her threat to shoot him. Soon after, she relates her cowardice to his declaration of Thea's stupidity. And, at the apex of tension in this scene, Hedda reverses their roles and tells him that she will confess to him. The stage directions detail her posture as she leans close to Løvborg and speaks softly without looking him in the eyes. She declares that her "worst cowardice . . . that evening" was not her refusal to shoot him. The implication, of course, is that she now believes her sexual refusal was cowardly and that she wishes she had accepted his erotic offer, that it was merely her fear of society's condemnation, not her own desires, that impeded her.

Of course, even this confession sustains their relationship on the verbal level, in which the physical is stimulated but restrained, and Hedda makes that confession only after she has emphatically declared that while she does not love Tesman, she will not allow infidelity. The carefully measured syntax of Ibsen's original text balances her lack of love for Tesman with the impossibility of infidelity:

HEDDA: Love? That's good!

LØVBORG: Not love, then!

HEDDA: But no kind of unfaithfulness! I'll have none of that. (221)

Consider the references to restraint, confinement, and prohibition that sound in Hedda's language. The character of Hedda accepts the social and gender restraints imposed on her and vitalizes them in her desire to avoid the appearance of that which would be outside of the acceptable.

Hedda cannot write her own narrative because the very content of that psychic document, the material it would re-present, cannot be presented to her experience, except indirectly through Løvborg's representation. It is important that within Hedda's consciousness, life can be experienced only through representation; and her desire for Løvborg to kill himself as an *aesthetic* act is consistent with the fact that her most significant moments—those when she was most in touch with the world—she experienced through his representation, his translation of experience into narrative. Both Hedda and Thea believe that Løvborg has given them the most vital representation of the world they will have. In that sense, his language, whether spoken or written, is the instrument of their knowledge. Because they cannot experience the world directly, his mediation of the world becomes valuable to them. The ideology of Løvborg's vision attracts, even seduces, Thea, and there is clearly a sexual significance in that excitement; but that energy manifests itself in her response to the expansiveness of his ideas. Ibsen presents Hedda, of course, as indifferent to Løvborg's writing. She is not interested in the content of the recently published book or in the manuscript that falls into her hands. She reads nothing

Two faces of Hedda Gabler: *left,* Maggie Smith in the Ingmar Bergman production at the National Theatre, London, 1970, *photograph by Zoe Dominic; right,* Kate Mulgrew (with Dakin Matthews) in the Mark Taper Forum production, 1986, *photograph by Jay Thompson.*

of either. This indifference allows her to take her revenge on Thea by destroying the precious manuscript, and that indifference clarifies that her interest in Løvborg as narrator, as historian, is limited to his descriptions of his sexual adventures.

By killing himself as an aesthetic act, Løvborg would, in Hedda's imagination, give her an image of the world caught within a single moment that she could keep vivid in memory. Her questioning of Judge Brack about Løvborg's death expresses her wish that the static picture of her desire—the vision of Eilert lying dead with a gunshot wound in his temple—be clarified and made real in Brack's language. She doesn't necessarily desire that she herself see that situation directly. She realizes that this kind of experience, and the connection between her and Løvborg that her presence at that scene would suggest, is outside of her circumscribed world. However, she can experience that scene—the aesthetic vision of Løvborg's heroic suicide—through Brack's description. That is, she would experience the act and its scene as *representation*, not as experience. She could, therefore, perceive the suicide in the same way as a reader uses Goethe's narrative of Werther's suicide and lingering death—as an aesthetic object.

The competition between Tesman and Løvborg, both historians and evidently both potential candidates for the same professorship, aligns two different figures: the careful, methodical researcher and arranger, who focuses on a single aspect of a single moment in remote history, and the radical visionary capable of making large-scale generalizations about the future. As well, Tesman's work stands unwritten, tangible only in the raw material of historical prose, as the transcripts of archival documents that crammed his suitcase and the collections that remain unsorted. Tesman's specialization, the domestic arts or crafts of Brabant in the Middle Ages, demands that he collect a large number of objects. However, while the text refers several times to his *collection* and his need to work with it, organizing and arranging, none of these objects appears on the stage and none is identified specifically. This absence provides another instance in the play in which Ibsen keeps the material of the world outside of the scene that is displayed on the stage. Tesman's scholarship processes both the transcripts of the archival material he discovered, represented indirectly by the empty suitcase that held them, and his *collections* which we assume exemplify the craft objects that are his subject. The physical sense of these unseen artifacts, however, clarifies one difference between Løvborg's work and Jørgen's. The text defines Løvborg's work to be independent of the detritus of archives and collected artifacts and original in its ability to synthesize the past conceptually and project itself into the future. That is, Løvborg's work is narrative whereas Tesman's work remains at the level of transcriptions and mundane artifacts from the lives of ordinary people, unarranged and, as yet, untemporalized. Even as potential content, Tesman's unwritten book does not provide material that would be positioned chronologically within a story that would give his objects meaning.

When Jørgen Tesman returns from the all-night festivities, he tells Hedda about Løvborg's new manuscript. He confesses his envy for Eilert Løvborg's brilliance to Hedda: "One of the most remarkable books ever written, I'd almost say. . . . I sat and envied Eilert that he had been able to write something like that!" (236). Løvborg's work, therefore, defines, for Tesman, the possibilities of conceptualization that his own work cannot realize. Remember that when he first hears Løvborg describe the unpublished manuscript, Tesman declares that it would never have occurred to him to write about that subject. As he describes the moment when Eilert actually read him the manuscript, he conveys his excitement to Hedda. Here, in this situation in which Løvborg reads to Tesman at Brack's house, while the judge makes the final arrangements for the party, the text pictures another instance in which this young figure excites his listener with the words he speaks or reads while a third party busies himself nearby. In the other instances of Løvborg's storytelling—his narration of sexual adventure to Hedda, his sense of history and description of the world told to Thea—the seductiveness of his speech seems clear. It is almost impossible to think that his vision of the future does not hold an erotic charge for these listeners. Surely part of Jørgen's jealousy derives from the virility of Løvborg's language and ideas. In Tesman's description of the manuscript from the notes, the content of the book is more directly erotic. In the final published version of *Hedda Gabler*, Tesman's comments are generalized. Here again, Eilert's words, controlling a wide sweep of ideas, operate as instruments of seduction and excitation. When Tesman discovers that Hedda has destroyed that manuscript and accepts the falsehood that she has committed this crime for him, he sees himself—albeit falsely—for the first time as a part of Hedda's sexual experience. In his imagination, their relationship has appropriated the sexual energy that he experienced in Løvborg's narrative, although surely he would not express it in those terms. He mistakes the burning of Eilert's manuscript as an act of passion for him. In the same speech in which he declares that no one should ever learn that she burned these papers, he rejoices that she *burns* for him and wishes to share that knowledge with Aunt Julle. Tesman conflates his excitement about Løvborg's new book, his ironic identification with him (even through jealousy), his misconception of Hedda's motive as an erotic desire for him, and his happiness of the suggested proof of his virility in Hedda's hints of her pregnancy. The energy contained in the book and released in its destruction is erotic; however, as spectators of the scene in which Hedda burns the manuscript, we recognize that the sexual jealousy it manifests is hers. We recognize that the object she destroys represents for Hedda the tangible proof of Eilert's relationship with Thea.

The content of Løvborg's destroyed narrative remains inaccessible to the spectators of Ibsen's play; the slight manuscript—capable of being carried in a coat pocket—is present only in the inadequate, careful, and often deliberately obscuring secondhand reports of the listeners. And, of course, a disorganized version of this narrative is present in the fragmented notes for his dictation, preserved by Thea, whose transcription by the reconfigured pair, Thea and Jørgen, remains deferred until they have restored its narrative sequence. As theatrical objects, as properties, these notes exist in the stage picture, as the manuscript does as well, but as spectators we cannot read their words. And we recognize at some level that the writing we see is merely the product of whomever produced the properties used in the performance. While this text represents the strongest and most dangerous image of energy—both intellectual and sexual—as narrative or acts of narration, the play consistently keeps that image off-stage and the audience sees only its effect displayed in the remembered perception of the listeners. The play does not answer the question of whether Thea and Jørgen have either the memory or the imagination to rebuild Eilert's narrative from these fragments. Ibsen's draft material contains a bitterly ironic speech for Hedda obviously thought out for inclusion in act 4: "When H. talks to B. in Act 5 about those two sitting there trying to batch the manuscript together without the spirit being there, she bursts out laughing.—Then the piano-playing—then—d—."[2] The absence of this speech in later drafts reflects a process in which Ibsen substituted direct action for the characterization of behavior in the speech of others. That is, the playwright allows the audience to make that mediated judgment rather than using the figure of Hedda to voice that attitude. This deletion, of course, allows the text to represent Hedda focused on her own circumstances and move toward her final act with a sharper focus.

In terms of the paradigmatic model I have emphasized throughout this chapter, I would like to clarify the implicit stage picture of the final moments. Thea and Tesman are engaged in *reconstructing* the Løvborg manuscript—that crucial artifact—from the fragments of his notes. This theoretical narrative deals with the future as the implementation of a unique, modern relationship between the sexes. Therefore, like the stories that Løvborg told Hedda and the historical narrative that he dictated to Thea, the narrative has a highly erotic content. However, Ibsen withholds that information from us in the published version of the play. Thea and Tesman work, intimately bound to each other, enacting the Thea/Løvborg relationship self-consciously:

> HEDDA: . . . Isn't this stange for you, Thea? Now you're sitting here with Tesman . . . as you used to sit with Eilert Løvborg.
>
> MRS. ELVSTED: Oh yes, oh God . . . if only I could inspire your husband in the same way.
>
> HEDDA: Oh, I expect it will come . . . in time.

TESMAN: Yes, d' you know what, Hedda . . . it really does seem to me that I'm beginning to feel something of the sort. But you go and sit down again, now, with Mr. Brack. (267)

After the disturbance of Hedda's piano playing, Tesman suggests to Thea that she move to Frøken Julle's home, where he could come in the evening to work with her. Curiously, Tesman posits another situation in which two would converse with the presence of a third—here, Frøken Tesman—somewhat outside of the complicity of the two. As well, in this image, Thea Elvsted becomes the substitute for the invalid Aunt Rina as the figure for whom Frøken Tesman would dedicate her energy.

In a lapse of decorum, antithetical to his concern about Løvborg calling upon Hedda during his absence, Tesman asks the judge to entertain Hedda in the evenings he works with Thea. Here he inadvertently contributes to putting her in jeopardy with Brack. At this moment, of course, the gunshot shatters the structure of this future.

While there are several instances in *Hedda Gabler* in which characters speak of events in narrative statements, these revelations of the distant past or immediate history are always partial and elliptical. One of the techniques of Ibsen's realistic style is the gradual accumulation of a detailed image of the past, and the formation of a significant revision of the past in the consciousness of his central character constitutes a principal part of the action he dramatizes. Here the playwright violates a personal convention that determines the structure of almost all of his dramas. The principal narrative consciousness in this text rests in the psyche of Eilert Løvborg, who assumes a position slightly off center in the organization of the drama. This shift of emphasis results in the diminishing of a central aspect of one of Ibsen's primary images: the aesthetic or narrative project. In other terms, we could describe this project as the hero's mission. Consider, for example: Brand's ministry, shaped in the language of the demand of the absolute; Julian's attempt to encompass a comprehensive vision of reality; the master builder's sequence of building churches to glorify God, homes to enclose happy people, the union of the two in his own new house, and the final, illusory "castles in the air"; Rosmer's educational mission; Allmer's philosophical project; Borkman's capitalistic empire; and Rubek's sculpture. In each of these vocational projects, the hero works through a sequence of self-formative conceptualizations that relate the project to highly specific interpretations of reality. Eilert Løvborg's vocational project, which, in definition, becomes the most comprehensive and ambitious of all of the Ibsenian vocational objectives, constitutes a historical evaluation of human history to the present and a visionary plan for the future. However, in this drama, which focuses on the female, the playwright shifts the vocational, narrative project to the edge of the spectator's focus. As a consequence, the text withholds crucial information about Løvborg's writing. In chapter 4, I cited that segment from the notes on *Hedda Gabler* that relate Eilert's manuscript to a new vision of society that builds on the comradeship of the sexes. The published version of the text, of course, suppresses that connection. Significantly, Ibsen elected to make the manuscript an important physical artifact, which with the pistols, is one of the two most functionally significant physical objects on the stage; and yet the playwright deliberately emptied out the principal ideological content of that physical image.

Løvborg's verbal representation of reality takes three forms in the language of the play: the documentation of his sexual experiences in the extended conversations with Hedda that exist in the play only as referents; his recently published book, which he claims he wrote to please his potential audience and regain his reputation as a scholar; and his new manuscript that, according to his description, manifests his true vision and, according to Tesman's evaluation, constitutes "one of the most remarkable" books ever written. These pages—tangible in the manuscript Hedda burns and potentially available again in the fragmented notes Thea has maintained—work with the dueling pistol as the critical stage properties that turn the plot. Løvborg's narrative remains outside of the play even though it is a critical physical object of the drama in performance, the key instrument whose loss makes Løvborg's hysterical rejection of Thea and fatal attack on Diana plausible. This

important ellipsis removes the connection between Eilert's earlier relationship with Hedda—their *comradeship*—and the ideological substance of the lost manuscript. If that connection remained intact, the
past relationship and Løvborg's idealized projection of the future
would relate. Hedda's renunciation of that relationship—her fear of
scandal and retreat from sexuality—would have held a different content. Their relationship would have been more intellectual, more ideological, less idiosyncratic, less a psychological phenomenon. The text,
as it stands, emphasizes the psychic fragility of both Hedda and
Løvborg and diminishes the significance of their relationship and its
alignment with any kind of comprehensive sociological vision of the
future. Hedda maintains no ideology, and the text of the drama suppresses the ideas of Løvborg's progressive vision, both by destroying it
in the action of the play and by refusing to let its content enter the
dialogue. If that content had remained, we would recognize that the
primary model of heterosexual union, the comradeship upon which the
vision of the future is based, would be the relationship of Hedda Gabler
and Eilert Løvborg.

In the draft material, of course, the possibility for a different
drama exists: A text in which the central artifact, the handwritten
manuscript of Løvborg's book, is identified as a vision of the future
based on the true comradeship of male and female; and the two figures
whose magnetism defines the poles of attraction in this drama would
figure as the prototype of the future (see the Oxford edition, 489).
Ibsen's final text, however, removes that description of the book and
poses a different relationship between the two. Hedda Gabler does
relate to Løvborg as the instrument through which the world is represented to her, but her vision of the world does not encompass the kind
of conceptualization that Løvborg works out in his writing, or in his
dictation to Thea. Hedda's interest in Løvborg focuses on a different
kind of representation, his confessions of sexual activity. This interest,
which encompasses her "idealized" image of him as a Dionysian figure, displays her radical disinterest in a more inclusive narrative; or,
more accurately, the narrowness of her focus plays itself out in the
limited range the playwright's text provides for her.

9

The Rhetoric of Circumlocution

In a scene of act 2 Hedda and Løvborg sit in the front drawing room and talk while Jørgen and Brack chat, drink, and smoke in the inner room. The former friends leaf through an album of pictures from the Tesmans' wedding trip in order to mask their real conversation. Here Hedda and Løvborg maintain two dialogues: a rather formal exchange for the benefit of Tesman and Brack and a frank and intimate review of their previous relationship. As they discuss the nature of their conversations several years earlier in General Gabler's drawing room, they focus on Løvborg's revelations of his licentious behavior. Løvborg claims that in the process of making these disclosures, he washed "himself clean" in an act analogous to religious confession. As I noted, he associates these reports with the concept of expiation through story-telling. The term he uses in the original text denotes both narrative discourse and religious confession. Hedda describes these afternoon conversations differently in her claim that they provided the only means by which she could access a world that was otherwise closed to her. However, both agree that they approached the problematic content of these stories by indirection. Note the way in which they speak of the uses of circumlocution in the following section of dialogue.

LØVBORG: . . . —and then when I used to confess to you . . . ! Told you things about myself that none of the others knew at that time. Sat there and admitted that I'd been out on the razzle for whole days and nights. For days on end. Oh, Hedda . . . what power was it in you that forced me to reveal all those things?

HEDDA: Do you think it was a power in me?

LØVBORG: Well, how else can I explain it? All those . . . those round-about [subtly disguised] questions you'd put to me . . .

HEDDA: And which you were so quick to understand . . .

LØVBORG: That you could sit there and ask like that! Quite confidently!

HEDDA: Roundabout [subtly disguised] questions, if you please.

LØVBORG: Yes, but confidently all the same. To cross examine me about . . . about all those things!

HEDDA: And that you could answer me, Mr. Løvborg. (222–23).

Løvborg emphasizes that his confessions were provoked by her questioning and, thereby, suggests that she provided both the impulse and the form for his revelations. He identifies the energy of that questioning as a force within her that demanded his answers. Here, some years later, they discuss the boldness with which she interrogated him; and Hedda reminds him that her questions never employed language that was inappropriate, indecorous. They agree that Hedda approached the subject of Løvborg's sexual adventures by framing her questions in a process of subtle indirection.

The rhetorical strategy of circumlocution directs much of the dialogue of this play. All of the characters discuss topics without using a vocabulary that names the actualities of certain significant subjects: Hedda's pregnancy; Løvborg's alcoholism, his sexual behavior; the specifics of Rina's illness; Brack's sexual liaisons, his attempts to establish a continuing sexual relationship with Hedda; Diana's prostitution; Thea's willingness to build an illicit liaison with Eilert; the financial threat of Tesman's possible failure to receive the professorship. While these subjects constitute the narrative material of this text and the substance of much of its dialogue, the nouns that would name these activities remain unspoken. In this rhetorical convention, the speaker embeds significant information in language that, on the surface, appears to mask the unspeakable or hidden but actually translates it into forms that may be spoken without violating social codes. While circumlocution allows the speaker to expose the existence of the unspeakable in the terminology of the accepted lexicon, the substitute language neutralizes and distances its content. Circumlocution manipulates a vocabulary that attempts to circumscribe the unspeakable within acceptable terms that isolate the object or event or activity: setting it apart as a transgression but hiding or occluding its specific content. To speak through this process of indirection and disguise puts the listener, and often the speaker as well, into an oblique relationship to the actual referents of statement. At times, circumlocution operates in situations in which both the speaker and listener know what is being discussed but communicate within the socially accepted prohibition against the practice of voicing certain words in public. At other times, the actual content of the subject remains hidden and the referent becomes therefore a generalized indiscretion identified as transgressive but undefined. This indirection of reference dislocates the content and puts the language into a tenuous relationship to the object, person, or behavior being discussed. Fact and supposition interact without being grounded in a clear relationship to each other. The specific reference of communication remains out of range, unseen, inaccessible, identified as present in the external world, but vague and unspecified and, in some sense, potentially more frightening in these unknown coordinates.

In *Hedda Gabler,* the circumlocution demanded by its social world diffuses the ostensible realism of the play at the same time in which its decorum of language attempts to replicate the absence of the offensive in the kind of everyday speech that would characterize the dialogue of two members of the upper middle class in a drawing room at the end of the nineteenth century. While the text renders the specific environment of this room in intricate detail, the world external to the play remains strangely indistinct. At this point, however, I need to examine specific circumlocutions that illustrate the relationship that the text of *Hedda Gabler* sets up between character and the external world and, correspondingly, between spectator and external world.

When Thea reports Løvborg's reformation to Hedda and Tesman in the first act, neither she nor the Tesmans assign a name or a descriptive adjective to the behavior Løvborg has renounced. Thea tells them that Løvborg has been serving as her stepchildren's tutor.

TESMAN: [*slightly incoherent*] But was he sufficiently . . . I don't [quite] know how to put it . . . sort of . . . well, regular enough in his life and habits so that he could be trusted with . . . ? Eh?

MRS. ELVSTED: For the last two years, there's been nothing that anyone could hold against him.

TESMAN: Hasn't there really? Think of that, Hedda!

HEDDA: Yes, I'm listening.

MRS. ELVSTED: Nothing at all, I assure you. (187)

Here both Tesman and Mrs. Elvsted refer to Løvborg's former drunkenness by naming, albeit very generally, its opposite: suitable or regular habits, a recent record of behavior that holds nothing that could be used in criticism of him. I select this particular example because at this moment the text shows Tesman struggling—"I don't know quite how to put it"—to find the words to identify Løvborg's "unspeakable" past behavior in language suitable to use before Hedda and Thea. As the play develops, despite continued circumlocution, we gain some sense that Løvborg's indiscretion includes both alcoholism and sexual misbehavior. The text of the scene in which Hedda questions Thea and Thea reveals some of the details of her relationship with the reformed Løvborg contains Thea's revelation that "the shadow of a woman" stands between Løvborg and her. In an earlier draft of this dialogue Thea boldly declares that she knows that this woman is Hedda. The final version includes two telling circumlocutions. The first, of course, is Thea's tentative identification of this *woman* as the red-haired "singer," an identification that thinly disguises her function as prostitute; the second is Hedda's reinforcement of the substitution of Frøken Diana for the unnamed woman she recognizes is herself. The availability of the draft material allows us, therefore, to see the playwright's hand in removing that knowledge of Hedda's former relationship with Eilert from Thea's consciousness and allowing Hedda to manipulate the circumlocution that masks her identity as this shadow figure who once threatened Løvborg with a gun.

In act 2 Brack and Hedda play verbally with her description of being confined with Tesman in railway compartments on journeys in which she is subject to interminable conversations with the scholar, the "specialist," as she names him. Here both Hedda and the judge use the metaphor of the railway journey to speak of the continuity of her marriage, and they use the image of her "jumping out" to refer to the possibility of Hedda's leaving the marriage to form an extramarital sexual relationship. The reference to a third party who would join Hedda and Tesman in the compartment alludes to a second possibility, the maintenance of a potentially extramarital sexual relationship among one of the two original parties and the newcomer. This exchange demonstrates the skillful control with which both Hedda and Brack manage their sexual references within the safety of an almost-neutralized vocabulary. This specific interaction begins with Hedda's complaint of the boredom of conversation with Tesman. She has already introduced the figure of the railway journey with her husband, both as a metaphor for the marriage as a whole and as a literal reference to their recent journey.

BRACK: Well, then you jump out and move around a little, my lady.

HEDDA: I'll never jump out.

BRACK: Are you quite sure?

HEDDA: Yes, because there's always someone there who'll . . . —

BRACK: [*laughing*]. . . . Who'll look at your legs, you mean?

HEDDA: Exactly.

BRACK: Oh well, good Lord . . .

HEDDA: [*with a gesture of dismissal*] Don't like it [I won't tolerate that]. Then I'd sooner stay where I am . . . in the compartment. Two people alone together.

BRACK: Well then, if somebody else climbs into the compartment . . .

HEDDA: Ah, yes . . . that's quite another thing!

BRACK: A trusted and sympathetic friend . . .

HEDDA: . . . who can converse on all manner of lively topics . . .

BRACK: —and who's not in the least academic! [a specialist].

HEDDA: [*with an audible sigh*] Yes, that really is a relief. (208)

Somewhat earlier Brack has spoken of the special value of triangular relationships in which he is a "trusted" friend, more of the wife than the husband, in which he has the freedom of the house to come and go as he pleases. He notes the "convenience" that this relationship may hold among all three parties. Hedda, at this earlier point in the conversation, does not seem to read the sexual connotations of this triangle as acutely as when Brack suggests she jump off the metaphoric train. Here, when Brack guesses that what she fears is public perception, scandal—"Someone who'll look at your legs!"—his language, more direct, almost violates the complicity of the verbal contract. Translators often soften the impact of that line by using "ankles" rather than "legs." But this rare reference to a typically hidden part of the body clarifies the sexual meaning of Brack's language, a meaning that Hedda now recognizes. What Hedda appears to reject in this exchange is the public condemnation that she would experience if she were to leave the marriage with Tesman for a liaison with Brack. What she may suggest as a possibility in Brack's mind is the potentiality of a sexual liaison that is masked by the marriage with Tesman and Brack's position as the friend of both husband and wife. Of course, later, when Brack threatens to use his knowledge of Hedda's role in Løvborg's death to force her into a sexual relationship, she cannot accept that possibility because she would no longer be in control of her own body, her own experience.

The indirection of their dialogue leaves it unclear whether or not Hedda would accept a sexual relationship with Brack on her own terms. In part of the dialogue between Hedda and the judge that Ibsen deleted in his final version of the play, Brack expresses his keen dislike of children and the fact that in the past six months he has lost three "homes"—clearly, he speaks about liaisons with married women—because of the arrival of "intruders" who demand the attention of their mothers. In this version, therefore, Hedda, who denies the possibility of that happening in her case, may fear her pregnancy because of both its intrusion on her life in general and the potential loss of Brack in particular. In the final version of this text, the judge also speaks about becoming "homeless," but here the potential intruder is not a child but, rather, Løvborg.

> BRACK: ... Yes. I must admit I'd find it extremely awkward if this fellow were to become a constant visitor here. If this superfluous and ... unsuitable individual were to insinuate himself into ...
>
> HEDDA: Into the triangle?
>
> BRACK: Just so. For me it would be like becoming homeless.

Consider another example of the uses of circumlocution in the play. When Brack, in the fourth act, arrives to announce the death of Løvborg and the circumstances that frame it, he proceeds obliquely, glossing over the specifics of the wound, the location in which the incident occurred, and, as well, the fact that the young man is already dead. Later, alone with Hedda, he reveals that he used circumlocution to spare the feelings of Thea Elvsted. As he corrects her delusive image of Løvborg's death as an aesthetic act, we recognize, as well, that Brack reserves the specific information to exercise power over Hedda. She reconciles herself to the fact that Løvborg shot himself in the chest, asserting "Well ... the breast is good too," and soon Brack corrects her: "he was shot in the abdomen [groin]." This direct statement, countering both Hedda's romanticized vision and the text's insistence on circumlocution, disrupts this scene, sounding a shocking note that violates the decorum of this space and, thereby, exerts an extraordinary power. The directness of Brack's statement clarifies Hedda's loss of power to control the language spoken in her presence. The noun that Brack uses to specify the location of Løvborg's wound is *underlivet*. Translators usually use stomach, belly, abdomen, bowels for this term, which, as F. G. Nelson notes, was "an almost taboo word in the 1890s for a part of the anatomy somewhat closer to the sexual organs than the stomach."[1] Brack's use of this noun would sound a strident, unexpected note that would almost break the rhetoric of circumlocution as he pushes his perogatives with Hedda.

Brack's carefully spoken insistence on certain actual details of Løvborg's death keeps Hedda from assimilating Brack's answers into her own subjective vision of the event. In that sense, Brack's realism assures that her ultimate psychic circumlocution fails. Hedda's presence, up to this point, controls the language of the play; and even though she desires knowledge, her fear of social condemnation and her subsequent loss of authority manifests itself in the decorum of her drawing room. Ibsen's representation of Hedda's character combines her desire to know the world and her fear of public perception. These conflicting impulses provide the central irony of the play. Until this point, reality invades the environment of Hedda's drawing room only through the sanitized language of what society determines appropriate and what Hedda will allow. The relative directness of Brack's description, even with its obvious occlusions, invades this protected space and destroys the image Hedda attempted to create with her illusory power over Løvborg. When she receives the information Brack discloses in its more undisguised form, that knowledge marks out the impossibility of her situation and makes her death a more attractive alternative.

The rhetoric of circumlocution in *Hedda Gabler* aligns with another technique with which this text organizes its dialogue: the substitution of interrogation for narration. Characters in this play do not reveal material through the convention of narrative recitation. Here the critical information is revealed through a sequence of questions and answers. Consider, for example, the circumstances of Thea's arrival in town, Hedda's response to the honeymoon, the reconstitution of Eilert's life, both Tesman's and Brack's version of the event of the party, and the revelation of Løvborg's death. These reports are not driven by a narrator's impulse to reveal but rather by the interrogator's curiosity. The carefully released units of information manifest the energy of repression more than of expression because the impulse to gain information comes from the questioner, and the person who discloses the information releases only enough to satisfy the immediate demand of the interrogation. As well, the questioner, who stands in partial knowledge, directs the sequence of the exposition and, for the most part, limits or extends its boundaries from a subjective, highly personal motive rather than from a desire for an objective clarification of the whole action. Hedda's questioning of Thea keeps the focus of Thea's revelations on the nature of her relationship to Løvborg and his difference from Elvsted. When Brack first offers the information on Eilert's injury, after a curious delay, he responds to Tesman's demands, then Thea's, and then Hedda's. His elliptic answer avoids direct response to Tesman's question about the source of his knowledge; he replies: "Through the police, a . . . man I had to see." Later, in private conversation with Hedda, he reveals the information that threatens her with scandal and puts her under his power. However, even here, Hedda's questions direct the revelation; and, as spectators, the only facts that we learn about Løvborg's death relate to the discrepancies between its circumstances and Hedda's idealized vision of what it should have been. Whether the gun discharged accidentally in a struggle between Løvborg and Diana, or Løvborg lost the gun in this struggle, or Diana deliberately took the gun and shot him remain questions that Brack assumes will be revealed only in the interrogation of the trial. In the play itself, these questions remain unanswered.

Brack arrives in the Tesman's drawing room in the afternoon of the fourth act to report the incident of Løvborg's shooting. In formal terms, his action corresponds to the function of the messenger in fifth-century tragedy. That is, this character reports the pathos, as the conventional messengers detail the encounter between Eteocles and Polyneices in Aeschylus's *Seven against Thebes*, the suicide of Jocasta and the self-blinding of Oedipus in Sophocles' play, or Agave's killing of Pentheus in Euripides' *Bacchae*. However, in the classic form of this convention of reporting the tragic act that takes place offstage, the messenger's recitation uses its language to reify a material scene that cannot, by theatrical practice, become part of the physical scene represented by the stage. In fifth-century tragedy, the detailed language of the narrative substitutes for the physical revelation of the forbidden scene. Language, therefore, both reveals and, as a representation and mediation of the scene it narrates, bars the reality of that scene, as action, from invading the protected space of the theater itself. In Ibsen's modern version, Brack does not, of course, narrate this *pathos;* he releases segments of disguised or neutralized data by responding to questions. While he is driven to reveal the general news of Løvborg's injury and death by his own motives, the scene dramatizes Brack's suppression of all but the necessary details he has come to report. The texts of classical tragedy enclose the messengers' narrations in the form of single discourses that represent the voices of direct witnesses. Because this revelation takes the form of an interrogation that Brack cannot control, the theatrical moment represents a character whose energy is spent repressing information as much as exposing it. As well, we learn that Brack conveys information that he, himself, has gained through his interrogation of the police. We are distanced from the offstage event by hearing an interrogation of an interrogation. Consequently, as spectators, subject, as Hedda herself is to the censorship of Brack as well as to the limitations of his knowledge of the event, we never receive a full and unequivocal report of the circumstances of Løvborg's shooting.

The play *Hedda Gabler* and the character Hedda Gabler are both bound by a rhetoric of circumlocution. The world outside of the bounds of the Falk Villa is one of sexual excess and economic jeopardy: drunkenness, prostitution, financial recklessness, the arbitrariness of civil and academic bureaucracies, the exploitation of women, and the threat of poverty. One of the principal characters of the play dies from an accidental gunshot wound in an apartment that functions, at least temporarily, as a brothel. Another principal clearly is familiar with the prostitute involved in the incident, and he attempts to force the heroine into an illicit sexual relationship through blackmail. The relationship he proposes appears to replicate a series of liaisons that he has already enjoyed with women of equivalent social standing in the community. The heroine, defined by herself as unwilling to jeopardize her social position in any direct involvement with the world external to the codes of her class, is drawn to experiences in which she can have some access to that world through the secondhand reports of participants. In some sense, the play represents the failure of circumlocution in that Hedda Gabler cannot, ultimately, protect herself from the loathsomeness, the repulsiveness, the ultimately farcical nature of the reality outside of her immediate environment. The world external to her tightly circumscribed circle attracts Hedda and stimulates her to perceive her restricted experience as both a safe social haven and a stifling constriction. Her economic desperation forces her to expand her limited world to include the bourgeois Tesman and his family, and she attempts, unsuccessfully, to impose the behavior of her own circle upon the less sophisticated conventions of middle-class life. Her attraction to both Løvborg and Brack and to the freedom commanded by males directs her involvement with that forbidden male world, an involvement that destroys her control of the Falk Villa.

As spectators, we perceive the world external to the strictly defined limits of the Falk Villa—the world forbidden to Hedda—only through the language that can be spoken in Hedda's presence. After the initial expository scenes among Frøken Julle, Berte, and Tesman, Hedda's presence dominates the space. With the exception of these expository conversations and the very brief exchange between Thea and Berte at the beginning of act 3 while Hedda sleeps, we are privy to no extended conversations that take place outside of her hearing. Hedda is the only character in the play who never leaves the Falk Villa. The dynamics of the world external to that space may be reported to the Falk Villa, but those reports come within the language acceptable to this figure; the only information that intrudes is that which she allows. Hedda, of course, does not originate that restraint. Society, not this heroine, determines what may and what may not be spoken in her presence. Her desire for access to the world forbidden to her, demonstrated in her questioning of Eilert years before, comes into conflict with her equally strong demand to operate within the rules of the society that would forbid her the knowledge or experience she seeks. Consider, for example, that, within the realistic terms of the play, Brack is involved in the specific subcommunity that surrounds Diana; he has knowledge of her activities and of whom she invites, and he speaks as though he is familiar with her physical strength. His knowledge of Eilert Løvborg, both in the present and in the past, suggests his own more discreet participation in the world in which the younger man disgraced himself. Hedda herself exercises the obvious circumlocution of "lively" when she refers to the alcoholic and possibly sexual excesses of Brack's parties, but she limits the discussion of that activity to the euphuistic adjective. When she expresses the desire to be present at Brack's bachelor party as an *invisible* observer, she realizes that her actual presence would never be allowed, and, as well, recognizes that her presence would disallow the very events she wishes to observe. At its most innocent level, the party would include exclusively male conversation. At no point in this drama do we have conversation that takes place between males without the presence of a female. Consequently, as spectators, we share the limits of the kind of knowledge that would be granted the women in the text. This fact may constitute the most important aspect of the language of *Hedda Gabler.*

I noted the alignment between the rhetoric of circumlocution and the substitution of interrogation for narration. Hedda's final questioning of Brack holds its own ellipsis. She never questions his involvement in the circumstances of Eilert's death, the source of his knowledge, or the specifics of his information about Diana. Her refusal to place him within that world directly limits the form of her questions and exercises the tacit understanding that he can partake of that world and yet within the discretion of society remain—in language—outside of it. However, Hedda's unwillingness to open the questions to Brack's involvement limits our knowledge of that involvement.

When Brack implements his ultimate strategy—using the fact that he has knowledge that once revealed would bring scandal upon Hedda—he presents a short narrative in which he describes the potential scene at court in which Hedda would be interrogated about giving Løvborg the gun.

BRACK: . . . You will [would] of course be required to go into the witness box. Both you and Mademoiselle Diana. She will have to
explain how the event took place. Whether the wound was
inflicted accidently or deliberately. Was he about to pull the
pistol out of his pocket in order to threaten her? And did it
then go off? Or did she seize the pistol out of his hand, shoot
him down, and then stick the weapon back in his pocket? I
wouldn't put it past her. She's a spirited wench, is this Mademoiselle Diana [she's a very strongly built girl, this same Miss
Diana].

HEDDA: But all this revolting business has nothing to do with me.

BRACK: No. But you will be obliged to tell the court why you gave
Eilert Løvborg the pistol. And what inference will be drawn
from the fact that you did give it to him?

HEDDA: [*lowers her head*] That's true. I didn't think of that.

BRACK: Well, fortunately, there's nothing to fear so long as I keep
silence. (266)

Here, in this hypothetical, potential interrogation, Hedda would not
be in control of the questions and could not demark the limits they
impose or extend. The alternative to this loss of control, of course, is
her suicide.

Hedda's world is circumscribed by what society determines can
be spoken and enacted in her presence. The representation of the
world in the text itself is limited to what can be spoken and what can
be displayed in Hedda's presence. Because of this fact and because
Hedda herself, in Ibsen's characterization, does not possess a narrative
consciousness, the text of the play occludes critical narrative detail.
The past determines the present in the play as much as in Ibsen's other
realistic dramas, but much of that determining material remains outside of the spectator's reach. As I've noted, the working notes and
preliminary dialogue for the drama include a great deal more specific
narrative exposition, including the fact that Hedda's anxiety about her
social position derives at least in part from experiencing General
Gabler's disgrace. Many specific references to the past do not occur in
the dialogue of the finished play, and the details of the general's history

and the explanation for the fact that Hedda is apparently left no property and few personal possessions remain unclarified. In this play, the nature of much of the past, which contains sexual indiscretion, combined with the fact that much of that material is "unspeakable," demands that it be revealed through circumlocution. A significant part of the history that these dramatic figures confront and suffer cannot be addressed directly; and because the text reveals that unspeakable history in dialogue, dialogue that operates with content suppressed and through indirect referentially and shared codes, we spectators do not have sufficient access to the details that would stand as referents to the oblique allusions we hear. Consequently, the play itself assumes a dislocated, oblique relationship to a sense of reality despite the fact that it sustains a realistic surface.

Michael Meyer writes that the early criticism of performances of *Hedda Gabler* claims that this play is "the least Norwegian of Ibsen's plays" and makes no references that would tie it specifically to Christiania (Oslo) rather than any other continental capital. Meyer continues by noting William Archer's conflicting claim that the play is based upon Ibsen's image of the Norwegian city. Ibsen's text situates the play geographically in a combination of highly generalized reference and a few subtle details.[2] We know, for example, that the Tesmans arrive from "abroad" by steamer; and Thea Elvsted has come to town by train, from "*der oppe*," a remote provincial location. Tesman's rhetorical question in which he wonders how "she can stand it up there [*der oppe*]" suggests the provinciality and possibly primitive atmosphere of the area that Thea shares with Elvsted and then Løvborg. The research nature of the Tesmans' honeymoon suggests that the couple spent time in Belgium since Jørgen's subject is the folk crafts of Brabant in the Middle Ages. Tesman refers to archives but does not specifically identify their location. Nor does the text name the university that awarded him a doctorate, situating this institution generally as "abroad" and "down there." The only specific references to Tesman's itinerary relate to the Southern Tyrol. He refers to the effects of the Tyrolian atmosphere on Hedda; and, in her use of the photograph album, she makes specific reference to the Ortler range outside of Meran, the Dolomites, the Brenner Pass, and the Val d'Ampezzo. In Ibsen's preliminary notes, Tesman remarks that when they were in Gratz (Graubünden, Sweden), Hedda refused to visit her relatives. But this comment is removed in the final version.

The text details a large, distinguished one-story house. Ibsen's description of the house and his references to its spatial arrangement form a clear image of a substantial nineteenth-century residence typical of Oslo. This kind of one-story structure would arrange its rooms on an axial basis divided by a center hall. On either side of this hall, the rooms would open one upon the other in sequence. *Hedda Gabler* uses this idiosyncratic structure of sequencing rooms in the representation of a drawing room that opens onto an inner room that, in turn, gives access to the "two empty rooms that stand between [the] . . . back sitting room and Hedda's bedroom." The sense of Hedda's bedroom, the site of overt sexuality in the relationship between Tesman and Hedda, remains insulated from the space the stage displays. This formal drawing room, with the slipcovers removed from its furniture, functions as Hedda's everyday sitting room, to the surprise of Frøken Tesman. The idea of situating the action of the play in the most formal and public space of the former Falk Villa reinforces the kind of language spoken in *Hedda Gabler.*

In the final moments of the play, Hedda responds to Tesman's plan of working with Thea at his aunt's each evening by asking him what she shall do "out here." This reference, in combination with Brack's practice of walking from his rooms to the Falk Villa and coming *up* the back way, suggests that this house stands somewhat outside of the town on a elevated site, physically removed from the crucial events that take place during the time of the play. The draft version of the dialogue between Brack and Hedda at the opening of act 2 include a reference to the gardens and to the terrace outside the French doors where Hedda has been out only a "little." Brack here notes that the "lovely" view includes a vista over the fjord and the islands. In the final version, which circumscribes Hedda's world even more, Ibsen removes her movement out onto a terrace. The conversation between Thea and Hedda sets out a time scheme that includes

Thea's employment at the Elvsted's five years earlier and Eilert Løvborg's residence "up there" for the past three years. Hedda and Tesman identify the specific moment of the play as well into September, and since Frøken Julle notes that they married almost six months earlier, this time frame would set the wedding in March. Hedda's conversation with Brack relates to his going "in another direction" and being unavailable as her escort the summer before this late winter wedding. The death of General Gabler is given no specific time. Hedda's conversations with Løvborg, in the presence of the general in the Gabler home, had to take place at least three years earlier, before his residence in the provincial region he shares with Thea. Thea's relationship with Tesman, as well, was at least five years earlier, before she left the town to take up residence at the Elvsted's. Hedda's relationship with Tesman does not predate the summer of the previous year.

Within its ostensible realism, the play proceeds with an almost-classical brevity of detail about its characters; the significant data with which the play operates concerns the limited field of Hedda's drawing room and the dynamics of the interactions that take place there. The membrane between that field of play and the outside world limits what we, as spectators, can see and hear directly. That membrane, of course, is epithelial. The world outside does intrude and destroy through the contaminating presence of those who leave and reenter. But the off-stage presence of that external world is always mediated through the indirect language the text voices. *Hedda Gabler* represents a world in which only men and those women who exist outside of accepted society may confront the pleasures and dangers of that mundane reality firsthand. Only these figures can speak the words that name the phenomena of that world directly. Only men in the company of other men may speak without the indirect reference that marks the language we hear in the Falk Villa. Ibsen's text, however, does not extend its scene outside of those boundaries, and we hear no conversations solely among men. The world external to this drawing room remains as inaccessible to us as it does to Hedda. That is, the same restrictions that circumscribe the experience of women in Hedda's moment, station, and place in history limit our perception as well.

The Rhetoric of Circumlocution

The final moment shatters the membrane between this drawing room and the world outside, as Hedda violates the rhetoric of circumlocution and speaks through the transgression of her suicide. However, that shocking performance may constitute only a temporary instability as those who witness it translate its physical gesture into a kind of narrative, spoken in the particular circumlocutions with which they are comfortable.

Notes and References

1. The Historical Moment

1. Erich Auerbach, *Mimesis*, trans. Willard Trask (Princeton: Princeton University Press, 1953), 459. Originally published in German (Berne: Francke, 1946).

2. Gay Gibson Cima, "Discovering Signs: The Emergence of the Critical Actor in Ibsen," *Theatre Journal* 35 (March 1983),18. The intellectual and moral sympathy evident in these actresses contrasts to the refusal of Hedwig Niemann-Raabe, the German actress who, in 1880, refused to act the original ending of *A Doll's House* on the grounds that she would not abandon her own children. Ibsen capitulated by writing a different ending in which Nora is forcibly kept from leaving by Torvald and ends the play by collapsing in front of the children's bedroom. Ibsen declared that he wrote the revised ending as an expedient to keep his text, unprotected by copyright in Germany, from being corrupted by other hands. See Michael Meyer, *Ibsen: a Biography* (Garden City, N.Y.: Doubleday, 1971), 459–60.

3. George Bernard Shaw, appendix to *The Quintessence of Ibsenism*, included in *Shaw on Theatre*, ed. E. J. West (New York: Hill and Wang, 1958), 5.

4. See Charles R. Lyons, *Henrik Ibsen: The Divided Consciousness* (Carbondale and Edwardsville: Southern Illinois University Press, 1968), 164–66.

5. *Ibsen: Letters and Speeches*, ed. Evert Sprinchorn (New York: Hill and Wang, 1964), 291–92.

6. George Bernard Shaw, "The Technical Novelty in Ibsen's Plays," from *The Quintessence of Ibsenism* (London: Faber, 1913), 171–84. See reprint in Charles R. Lyons, ed., *Critical Essays on Henrik Ibsen* (Boston: G. K. Hall, 1987), 33.

2. The Importance of the Work

1. Lyons, *The Divided Consciousness*, xxiv–xxv.

3. Critical Reception

1. Lyons, *Critical Essays on Henrik Ibsen*, 3.

2. Meyer, *Ibsen: A Biography*, 644.

3. Henry James, "On the Occasion of *Hedda Gabler*," *New Review*, June 1891, 519–30. Reprinted in Michael Egan, ed., *Ibsen: The Critical Heritage* (London: Routledge & Kegan Paul, 1972), 243. Note the discussion of James's review in Gay Gibson Cima, "Discovering Signs: The Emergence of the Critical Actor in Ibsen," *Theatre Journal* 35 (March 1983),16. Cima's article directed me to reread James's comments.

4. At Bergen Ibsen staged several of Scribes's plays, including the famous *Une verre d'eau* (*A Glass of Water*), and learned their structure despite his disdain for them.

5. Shaw, *The Quintessence of Ibsenism*.

6. Aurélien Lugné-Poë, *Ibsen* (Paris: Rieder, 1936).

7. George Bernard Shaw, *Collected Letters, 1874–1897*, ed. Dan H. Lawrence (New York: Dodd, Mead, 1965), 292.

8. Meyer, *Ibsen: A Biography*, 646.

9. M. C. Bradbrook, *Ibsen, the Norwegian: A Revaluation* (1946), 2d ed. rev. (Hamden: Archon, 1966).

10. John Northam, *Ibsen's Dramatic Method* (London: Faber, 1948), 147–71.

11. Edward Said, "The Text, the World, the Critic," *Textual Strategies: Perspectives in Post-Structural Criticism*, ed. Josué Harari (Ithaca, N.Y.: Cornell University Press, 1979), 644.

12. Errol Durbach, *"Ibsen the Romantic"*: *Analogues of Paradise in the Later Plays* (London and Basingstoke: Macmillan, 1982), 52.

4. The Problem of Interpretation

1. Compare, for example, E. M. W. Tillyard's appropriation of Shakespeare's texts into the all-encompassing framework of an "Elizabethan World Order" in *Shakespeare's History Plays* (London: Chatto & Windus, 1959), 10–17, with Stephen Greenblatt's "Shakespeare and the Exorcists," *Shakespearean Negotiations* (Berkeley and Los Angeles: University of California Press, 1988), 94–128.

2. Robert Weimann, *Shakespeare and the Popular Tradition in the Theater*, ed. Robert Schwartz (Baltimore and London: Johns Hopkins University Press, 1978), xii.

3. Terry Eagleton, *Criticism and Ideology: A Study in Marxist Literary Theory* (London: Verso, 1978), 77.

4. "The saga is huge, cold, remote, self-sufficient, epic, quintessentially objective. . . . We cannot see the saga age except in this cold, epic light. . . . This dramatic treatment brings the saga age closer to reality, but that is exactly what should not happen. The statue does not gain by acquiring natural skin tints and real hair and eyes." From an article Ibsen sent to *Illustreret Nyhedsblad* on 17 April 1857, quoted in Meyer, *Ibsen: A Biography,* 149.

5. In the preface to the second edition (1883) of *The Feast at Solhaug,* Ibsen writes about the composition of *The Vikings at Helgeland:* "How far the details of that drama took shape, I am no longer able to say. But I remember perfectly that the two figures of which I first caught sight were the two women who in the course of time became Hjørdis and Dagny." Included in *Ibsen: Letters and Speeches,* 19–20.

6. Michael Fried, *Realism, Writing, Disfiguration: On Thomas Eakins and Stephen Crane* (Chicago and London: University of Chicago Press, 1987), 72.

7. I discuss this relationship between the conventions of character and theatrical scene in "Character and Theatrical Space," *Themes in Drama: The Theatrical Space,* vol. 9, ed. James Redmond (Cambridge: Cambridge University Press, 1987), 27–44.

8. Anthony Giddens, *Social Theory and Modern Sociology* (Stanford: Stanford University Press, 1987), 94.

5. Reconfiguration as Action

1. The Oxford Edition translates *kamarater* as "companions," but I prefer the stronger implication of comrades.

2. *Hedda Gabler,* trans. A. G. Chater, *From Ibsen's Workshop: Notes, Scenarios, and Drafts of the Modern Plays,* vol. 2 (New York: Charles Scribner's Sons, 1912), 383.

3. *From Ibsen's Workshop,* 2:401.

6. Social Structure

1. Eagleton, *Criticism and Ideology,* 78–79.

2. Ibid., 78.

3. *From Ibsen's Workshop,* 2:383.

4. I was pleased to note that Arup uses this term, *farce,* as that is how I translated the play in my working version of it.

5. *From Ibsen's Workshop,* 2:381.

6. Durbach, *"Ibsen the Romantic,"* 45.

7. This is my translation. The Oxford edition weakens the physical connotation here by translating the phrase as "spirited wench" (266).

8. I would not translate "*i eventyrlandet*" as "castles in the air" [*luftslottene*] because of the specific use of the actual image in *The Master Builder*. I would use the term *fantasy*.

7. Hedda Gabler (Tesman) and the Question of Character and Gender

1. I discuss this process, as a history, in "Ibsen's Drama and the Course of Modern Criticism," an essay that serves as the introduction to *Critical Essays on Henrik Ibsen*, 1–23.

2. A. C. Bradley, *Shakespearean Tragedy* (London: Macmillan, 1904).

3. E. H. Gombrich, *Art and Illusion: A Study in the Psychology of Pictorial Representation* (Princeton: Princeton University Press, 1960).

4. Muriel C. Bradbrook, *Ibsen the Norwegian: A Revaluation*, rev. ed. (1946 Hamden, Conn.: Archon Books, 1966), 116–18.

5. G. Wilson Knight, *Ibsen* (Edinburgh: Oliver & Boyd, 1962).

6. James Hurt, *Catiline's Dream: An Essay on Ibsen's Plays* (Urbana: University of Illinois Press, 1972), 153.

7. Durbach, "*Ibsen the Romantic*," 34.

8. See James Kerans, "Kindermord and Will in *Little Eyolf*," *Modern Drama: Essays in Criticism*, ed. Travis Bogard and William I. Oliver (New York: Oxford University Press, 1965), 192–208, reprinted in *Henrik Ibsen: Essays in Criticism*, 133–46.

9. See Errol Durbach's discussion of *Hedda Gabler* in "*Ibsen the Romantic*," 34–52, for an antithetical reading of the extent to which this play incorporates the Nietzschean paradigm.

10. Martin Esslin, *An Anatomy of Drama* (New York: Hill and Wang, 1976), 98.

11. For a discussion of the unity of the Ibsen canon and its dependence upon the structure of this sexual triad, see my first book on the playwright, *Ibsen: The Divided Consciousness*.

12. Ibsen's draft material for this play includes the following statement: "The pale, apparently cold beauty. Expects great things of life and the joy of life" (*From Ibsen's Workshop*, 2:381).

13. In the case of *Rosmersholm*, this statement needs some qualification since, after learning that her relationship with Dr. West was incestuous, Rebekka is unable to proceed with a sexual relationship with Rosmer. When he moves toward a sexual marriage, she takes over the repressive function and denies that possibility.

14. Luce Irigaray, *This Sex Which Is Not One* (Ithaca, N.Y.: Cornell University Press, 1985), 222.

9. The Rhetoric of Circumlocution

1. F. G. Nelson, review of Michael Meyer, trans., *Hedda Gabler and Three Other Plays, Scandinavian Studies* 34 (August 1962): 205.

2. Meyer, *Ibsen: A Biography,* 647.

Selected Bibliography

Primary Works

Editions

The Oxford Ibsen. Edited by James Walter MacFarlane. 8 vols. London: Oxford, 1962–. Well-translated editions of the plays that also contain useful supplementary information.

Ibsen: The Complete Major Prose Plays. Edited by Rolf Fjelde. New York: Farrar, Straus & Giroux, 1978. Clear and stageworthy translations.

Ibsen: Letters and Speeches. Edited by Evert Sprinchorn. New York: Hill and Wang, 1964. Useful assembly of Ibsen material.

Secondary Works

Biographies

Koht, Halvdan. *The Life of Ibsen*. Translated by Einar Haugen and A. E. Santainiello. 2d ed. rev. New York: Benjamin Bloom, 1971. English version of the 1928 Norwegian original that was revised in 1954. The standard biography until publication of the Meyer text.

Meyer, Michael. *Ibsen: A Biography*. Garden City, N.Y.: Doubleday, 1971. A richly detailed, finely researched study. Meyer's critical analyses, however are not particularly useful.

Selected Bibliography

Criticism

Bradbrook, M. C. *Ibsen the Norwegian: A Revaluation.* Hamden: Archon Books, 1966. Revision of 1946 study that attempts to replace the image of Ibsen the realist with an understanding of him as a poet in the theater.

————. "Ibsen and the Past Imperfect." *Contemporary Approaches to Ibsen.* Vol. 2. Edited by Daniel Haakosen. Oslo: Universitetsforlaget, 1970–71. Interesting treatment of the past in the general sequence of plays; particularly valuable in terms of *Hedda Gabler.*

Cima, Gay Gibson. "Discovering Signs: The Emergence of the Critical Actor in Ibsen." *Theatre Journal* 35 (March 1983):5–22. An excellent, well-researched article on a specific aspect of the history of Ibsen in performance.

Downs, Brian. *Ibsen: The Intellectual Background.* Cambridge: Cambridge University Press, 1946. A clear and incisive discussion of the ideologies informing Ibsen's plays.

Durbach, Errol, ed. *Ibsen and the Theatre.* London and Basingstroke: Macmillan, 1980. A collection of essays on text and performance by selected major figures.

————. *"Ibsen the Romantic": Analogues of Paradise in the Later Plays.* London and Basingstroke: Macmillan, 1982. An intelligent discussion that places Ibsen in the context of Romanticism and marks his antiromantic sensibilities.

Egan, Michael, ed. *Ibsen: The Critical Heritage.* London: Routledge & Kegan Paul, 1972. A very useful collection that documents Ibsen's reception.

Ewbank, Inga-Stina. "Ibsen's Dramatic Language as a Link between His 'Realism' and His 'Symbolism'." *Contemporary Approaches to Ibsen.* Vol. 1. Edited by Daniel Haakonsen. Oslo: Universitetsforlaget, 1965–66. Demonstrates the ways in which the realistic placement of metaphors provides a symbolic, but not allegoric, structure.

————. "Ibsen and the Language of Women." *Women Writing and Writing about Women.* Edited by Mary Jacobus. London: Croom Helm in association with Oxford University Women's Studies Committee, 1978. Excellent analysis of Ibsen's language and gender issues.

Finney, Gail F. *Women in Modern Drama: Freud, Feminism, and European Theater at the Turn of the Century.* Ithaca, N.Y.: Cornell University Press, 1989.

Hurt, James. *Catiline's Dream.* Urbana: Illinois University Press, 1972. General chronologically organized commentary on the plays from a psychoanalytic point of view based on R. D. Laing.

Johnston, Brian. *The Ibsen Cycle: The Design of the Plays from "Pillars of Society" to "When We Dead Awaken."* Boston: G. K. Hall, 1975. An interesting, if reductive, argument that attempts to show that Ibsen's writing is a direct sequential representation of Hegel's ideology.

Lyons, Charles R. *Henrik Ibsen: The Divided Consciousness.* Carbondale and Edwardsville: Southern Illinois University Press, 1972. Phenomenologically oriented study of selected major plays.

―――, ed. *Critical Essays on Henrik Ibsen.* Boston: G. K. Hall, 1987. Includes Northam's chapter on *Hedda.* Useful discussion of "Ibsen's Drama and the Course of Modern Criticism."

McFarlane, James Walter. *Ibsen and the Temper of Norwegian Literature.* Oxford: Oxford University Press, 1960. A fine critical survey of the plays.

Northam, John. *Ibsen's Dramatic Method.* London: Faber & Faber, 1953. A ground-breaking analysis of the relationship of dramatic language and the visual imagery realized in performance. Particularly useful in its discussion of *Hedda Gabler.*

Robins, Elizabeth. *Ibsen and the Actress.* London: Leonard and Virginia Woolf, 1928. Interesting commentary by a major American Ibsen actress who performed Hedda in London during the 1890s.

Tennant, P. F. D. *Ibsen's Dramatic Technique.* Cambridge: Cambridge University Press, 1948. Clear, formal analysis of Ibsen's functional structure.

Index

Absurdity. *See* Farce

Achurch, Janet, 4

Actors: identification with Ibsen's social program, 4–5

Aeschylus: *Seven Against Thebes,* 127

Agency: Human, character as, 86; as fallacy of intentionality, 29; and Ibsen's idiosyncracy, 40–41; *see also* Foucault, Michel; Giddens, Anthony

Antoine, Andre: and *Théâtre Libre,* 17; and *Théâtre de Menus Plaisirs,* 17

Apollonian. *See* Dionysian; Nietzsche, Friedrich

Archer, William, 18, 122

Arup, Jens, 64

Atemporality: of female self-formation, 101–2; of Hedda's consciousness, 84; isolation of characters in, 57

Auerbach, Eric: *Mimesis,* 4; on dated relevance of Ibsen plays, 38–39; on dialectic of text and history in Ibsen plays, 5; on self-interpreting function of text, 78

Avant-garde, 3, 18

Bardach, Emilie, 35

Beckett, Samuel: formation of character in, 77, 78, 80; dramatic representation in, 15; WORKS: *Not I,* 78; *Waiting for Godot,* 80

Bergman, Ingmar, 11, 83, 111

Bradbrook, Muriel C.: on absence of introspection in Hedda's character, 79; on Ibsen's dramatic language, 22; *see also* Criticism, New Criticism

Bradley, A. C.: mimetic concept of character, 75–76; lectures on Shakespeare, 75; *see also* Criticism, Mimetic

Brahm, Otto: and *Freie Bühne,* 17

Character: and Gender, 75–102; historically determined, 38–39; as hypothetical subject, 77; mediated by spectator, 77–78; as metonymic fragments, 77; as represented by actor, 76; as virtual whole, 77

Character criticism. *See* Mimetic criticism; A. C. Bradley

Child, symbolic, 25, 52; *see also* Sacrificed child

Chopin, Frédéric, mentioned, 53

Cima, Gail Gibson: on Ibsen actors, 4–5

Circle: image of, 73

Circumlocution, 42, 47, 48; through appearance of passion, 106; breaking the rhetoric of, 126; through euphuism, 130; by glossing over details, 125; by indirection, 119; through metaphor, 123; as moral restraint, 104; by naming oppo-

The Author

Charles R. Lyons is Margery Bailey Professor of English and Dramatic Literature at Stanford University, from which he earned his A.B., A.M., and Ph.D. He taught at the University of California, Berkeley, where he was vice chair and acting chair of Dramatic Art and associate dean, College of Letters and Sciences, before returning to Stanford as chair of the Department of Drama in 1973. His books include one of the earliest critical studies of Brecht published in English, *Bertolt Brecht: The Despair and the Polemic* (1968), *Shakespeare and the Ambiguity of Love's Triumph* (1970), *Henrik Ibsen: The Divided Consciousness* (1972), *Samuel Beckett* (1983), and *Critical Essays on Henrik Ibsen* (1987). His recent and forthcoming publications include several essays on the later plays and prose of Samuel Beckett and an extensive study of the representation of character, space, and time in a series of serious dramas from Aeschylus to Beckett.